Walk like Jesus Walked

Volume 2

Kingdom Culture

Loren VanGalder

Spiritual Father Publications

ISBN-13:   978-1-7336556-3-7

Contents

Introduction

Culture: The way of life of a particular people, especially as shown in their ordinary behavior and habits, their attitudes toward each other, and their moral and religious beliefs. (Cambridge Dictionary)

What is your culture like? What do you like about it? What bothers you about it? One culture is not better than the other; they are just different. But there is one perfect culture, the culture of God's kingdom. When we follow Jesus and walk together with him, we will walk as he walked and experience a new culture.

The Sermon on the Mount contains Jesus' most extensive teaching on kingdom culture. It is a radical message that goes directly against our secular culture—and popular church culture. Jesus contrasts the true disciple with the unbeliever and the "religious" person. We will see a huge contrast not only with the world around us, but also with many "Christians." You can expect the person who puts this message into practice to be characterized as:

- Different
- Weird
- Extreme
- Radical
- Counter culture

The Beatitudes: Who is the person God blesses?

The Sermon starts with the famous Beatitudes. *Beatitude* comes from the Latin Vulgate translation of the Greek word *makarios*. In English, it can be translated as blessed, happy, or fortunate, but it is far more than feeling happy; it is a life full of God's favor and blessing.

Before we read what Jesus says makes a person blessed, what would you say? I wanted to know—from among my predominantly Christian friends on Facebook—what others would say. Here are their responses.

God blesses the person who:

- Fears and honors him
- *I will bless those who bless you,*
  and whoever curses you I will curse;
  and all peoples on earth
  will be blessed through you (Gen. 12:3).
- Feeds and clothes the poor
- Loves him and obeys his commands
- Helps the "least of these" (Matt. 25:34-40)
- Honors him and is faithful
- Walks uprightly and loves their neighbor
- Is grateful
- Blesses others and blesses the Lord by being obedient in prayer, fasting and reading the Word
- Loves his neighbor as he loves himself
- Fears him, follows him, praises him, and obeys him

- Does not want to be "like" Jesus, but allows Jesus to live through him or her
- Does not tire of doing good
- Walks humbly before God and with others
- Belongs to him and is called by his name
- Chooses life (*Now choose life, so that you and your children may live.* Deut. 30:19)
- Obeys his Word
- Is a blessing to others
- God blesses whoever he wants to...it rains on the just and unjust
- Lives!
- Totally trusts him and surrenders to him
- He chooses to bless...all of us with the gift of his Son Jesus, dying for us while we were yet sinners
- Everyone

I am surprisingly impressed with my Facebook friends! Nobody mentioned things the world values, like money or success, but I do notice a tendency to think that it is our actions that elicit God's blessing. Jesus goes way deeper—and will have some surprises for you.

1

Blessed are the Poor in Spirit

Matthew 5:3

In Matthew 4, Jesus was just beginning his ministry. After being baptized by John and tempted in the wilderness by the devil, he called his first disciples. When it is time for God to raise you up, it can happen very quickly:

Jesus went throughout Galilee, teaching in their synagogues, proclaiming the good news of the kingdom, and healing every disease and sickness among the people. News about him spread all over Syria, and people brought to him all who were ill with various diseases, those suffering severe pain, the demon-possessed, those having seizures, and the paralyzed; and he healed them. Large crowds from Galilee, the Decapolis, Jerusalem, Judea and the region across the Jordan followed him (Matt. 4:23–25).

His miracles and teaching attracted multitudes, but Jesus wasn't interested in fame or crowds—he may have wanted to escape the multitude by climbing the mountain. Some curiosity seekers probably didn't bother following him, but those who did were challenged right here, at the beginning of his ministry, with a whole new concept of spirituality.

Just as Moses went up the mountain to receive the old covenant, Jesus went up the mountain to teach the new covenant, the culture of the kingdom. He cites the law numerous times and takes it to a deeper level, asserting himself as one with greater authority than Moses. The kingdom of God is a place of great blessing, but not necessarily in the ways we would expect.

The first Beatitude

[3] *"Blessed are the poor in spirit, for theirs is the kingdom of heaven.*

"God blesses those who are poor and realize their need for him, for the Kingdom of Heaven is theirs. (NLT)

"Blessed [spiritually prosperous, happy, to be admired] are the poor in spirit [those devoid of spiritual arrogance, those who regard themselves as insignificant], for theirs is the kingdom of heaven [both now and forever]. (AMP)

Jesus purposely gets our attention by shattering our expectations. We tend to think that the blessed person:

- Has great faith and walks in victory.
- Is very pious and religious.
- Is successful in ministry.

- Demonstrates impressive spiritual gifts like prophecy, healing, and miracles.
- Is full of the Holy Spirit and wisdom, and has abundant resources to share with others. In other words, rich in spirit.

Of course, those things are good, but Jesus says his kingdom belongs to the *poor* in spirit. Someone with great faith and a successful ministry can be poor in spirit, but it's harder!

What does it mean to be poor in spirit?

The New Living Translation says you realize your need for God. You have lost all confidence in your own righteousness and strength, and are acutely aware that you totally depend on Christ and the power of his Spirit. You have a humble and broken spirit, and recognize your bankruptcy (morally, spiritually, and even physically) before God. Being poor in spirit has nothing to do with fear or cowardice, or a false humility which denies the gifts and abilities God has given you.

Philosophers of the day didn't even recognize humility as a virtue, and, if we are honest, we tend to look down on the person who is poor in spirit. By nature, we are prideful and rebellious, valuing our independence. But God doesn't need people who are self-confident, well-educated, and possessing everything the world values. Paul had to learn spiritual poverty. He thought he was spiritually rich, but discovered that when he was weak, God could display his power.

This first beatitude offers great hope and encouragement. Jesus says that what is important to God is totally different than what we are accustomed to. It's not up to you! You don't have to act like you have it all together and are always walking in victory.

What does it mean to inherit the kingdom?

Jesus taught extensively about the kingdom. He said the kingdom is within us, as well as anywhere Jesus reigns and is Lord. He never wanted to establish a political kingdom, even though his disciples hoped he would overthrow the Romans and take the throne in Jerusalem. Unfortunately, many churches and pastors want to establish their own "kingdoms." Others are like the disciples and try to establish a Christian kingdom on earth.

Jesus uses the present tense: *Theirs **is** the kingdom*. The blessed person inherits the presence and government of Jesus in their life now. They may have nothing else in this world, but they have the King of kings. The blessing in each Beatitude is tasted now and fully experienced in the future. Jesus will return to this earth to establish his perfect kingdom, and the poor in spirit will inherit it. Those who already have their "kingdom" will be left outside. It was hard for the Pharisees, Zealots, or priests to enter the kingdom. Repentant, broken-hearted tax collectors and prostitutes joyfully embraced Jesus and his reign.

> *For this is what the high and exalted One says—*
> *he who lives forever, whose name is holy:*
> *"I live in a high and holy place,*

but also with the one who is contrite and lowly in spirit,
to revive the spirit of the lowly
and to revive the heart of the contrite.

(Isaiah 57:15)

The Laodicean church lost that humble attitude and was self-satisfied and superficial. They couldn't see their spiritual poverty:

You say, 'I am rich; I have acquired wealth and do not need a thing.' But you do not realize that you are wretched, pitiful, poor, blind and naked (Rev. 3:17).

It is easy for the long-time believer to become like the Laodiceans and feel they have "arrived" and are already rich.

Woe to the rich?

Luke 6 (the Sermon on the Plain) is often considered a parallel passage to the Sermon on the Mount. There are many similarities, and some significant differences; we don't know if both record the same "sermon." In Luke 6:20, Jesus simply says *Blessed are the poor*, confirming the priority of the poor in his ministry (Lk. 4:18). Luke 6:24 echoes what Jesus said several times about the wealthy: *But woe to you who are rich, for you have already received your comfort*. Luke's account gives a slightly different perspective on what our Lord values, but the basic idea is the same.

Do you feel poor in spirit? Rejoice! You are blessed! It is better to be poor in spirit than rich in spirit! Do you feel rich in spirit? Talk to the Lord and see if you need to repent and learn, like Paul, what is truly important to God.

2

Blessed are Those who Mourn

Matthew 5:4

Philippians 2 commands us to have the *mind* of Christ; we don't just *walk* like Jesus, we have to *think* like Jesus. The Beatitudes reveal what is important to Jesus, what brings joy to his heart, and who Jesus says is truly blessed. For the multitudes gathered on the mountainside to hear Jesus' teaching and see his miracles, these beatitudes were totally unexpected; they go against everything the world has taught us to value.

Those who mourn will be comforted

Blessed are those who mourn, for they will be comforted.

Isn't the mature Christian supposed to be full of joy, walking on the clouds in victory, and praising the Lord? The world seeks happiness at any cost and does everything possible to avoid pain and sadness. Western culture has downplayed mourning to the point that excessive grief at a funeral is frowned upon. After all, we Christians are quick to point out, "They are in a better place." Many of us don't even know how to mourn! The elaborate funerals of the past, or other cultures, make us uncomfortable.

Mourning implies the death of a loved one, or the loss of something very important:

- Things are *not* going well.
- God *didn't* heal your loved one.
- Your life seems to be falling apart.
- You may grieve lost love, lost hope, or lost opportunities.
- Your heart is broken.

Nobody welcomes that! But if there is nothing to mourn, there is no need for God to comfort you, and you will miss out on an important part of the Holy Spirit's ministry. Jesus was a *man of sorrows and acquainted with grief* (Is. 53:3).

- What are your feelings about grief? Are you acquainted with it?
- Is there something you are mourning right now?

- Did you feel that somehow you failed because that person died, or things turned out badly? Maybe others have suggested that it was due to your lack of faith or failure to pray enough.

Jesus says that God blesses the person who mourns, and mourning implies suffering. David danced, but he also cried. Psalm 56:8 says:

> You keep track of all my sorrows.
> You have collected all my tears in your bottle.
> You have recorded each one in your book.

Suppose you have a tender heart, full of compassion and God's love. In that case, you will mourn for the problems of this world, just as Jesus wept for his friend Lazarus (Jn. 11:35), and wept over unrepentant Jerusalem (Lk. 19:41). Tears reflect a reverent fear and submission to God, as seen in Jesus' example:

During the days of Jesus' life on earth, he offered up prayers and petitions with fervent cries and tears to the one who could save him from death, and he was heard because of his reverent submission (Heb. 5:7).

After recognizing our spiritual poverty in the first beatitude, we mourn our sin and failure to love and do the right thing, and our part in nailing Jesus to the cross. We are contrite and repentant.

In Luke, Jesus condemns the happy-go-lucky person: *Woe to you who laugh now, for you will mourn and weep* (Lk. 6:25). Why? Perhaps those who are laughing now are not serious about their sin and their relationship with God, or the needs of those around them. Does this mean we can never laugh? Of course not! But there is a common thread in these beatitudes of either having plenty now—but paying for it later—or allowing our struggles to draw us close to God, trusting him for a better future.

Do you have Jesus' heart? Would anyone call you a man of sorrows and acquainted with grief? Or are you laughing? It's not a sign of sin or weak faith to cry; it is part of being human. The real problem is being so hard-hearted, so insulated from others and their pain that you never grieve. If you are mourning, God knows! God cares! He is fully aware of every tear you shed. Whatever you might be mourning today, God promises to comfort you. Put aside your self-pity, self-condemnation, and confusion. God says the person who mourns is blessed. Can you actually believe that, and thank him for the painful circumstance? Let the Holy Spirit, the Comforter, touch the hurt in your heart today.

3

Blessed are the Meek

Matthew 5:5

If you are honest, do you really want to be meek? Do you see it as a blessing? Jesus said: *Blessed are the meek, for they will inherit the earth.*

"Blessed [inwardly peaceful, spiritually secure, worthy of respect] are the gentle [the kind-hearted, the sweet-spirited, the self-controlled], for they will inherit the earth. (AMP)

Can a real man be meek?

It may be great for a woman to be gentle and sweet-spirited (as in the Amplified Version), but it doesn't sound very manly. We might picture a meek man as an effeminate ninety-five-pound weakling.

Not very attractive. Yes, meekness has a definite negative connotation to men, which is confirmed by the way Peter uses the same Greek word in speaking to women (1 Pet. 3:4):

*You should clothe yourselves instead with the beauty that comes from within, the unfading beauty of a **gentle and quiet** (meek) spirit, which is so precious to God.*

But Jesus was meek. He entered Jerusalem humbly, on a donkey, and described himself as meek:

Take my yoke upon you and learn from me, for I am gentle and humble in heart, and you will find rest for your souls (Matt. 11:29).

What does it mean to be meek?

Webster defines meekness as: "Softness of temper; mildness; gentleness; forbearance under injuries and provocations. In an evangelical sense, humility; resignation; submission to the divine will, without murmuring or peevishness; opposed to pride and arrogance."

The meek person endures insult or injury without rising up in revenge. Instead, he turns the other cheek, trusting God to take care of him. The same word was used of an animal that was tamed, or a wild, worthless horse that had been broken, and could now be ridden or used for work. It was still just as strong, but its strength was under control. We submit our strength to God and exercise it under his control. Meekness is the opposite of arrogance.

Meekness in daily life

When we find ourselves in circumstances beyond our control or influence, we usually react with frustration, bitterness, or anger, but God calls us to respond in meekness. Our faith in God allows us to, trusting that he is sovereign, knows about the circumstances, and can work in them for our good. Meekness is not a resignation to fate or a passive and reluctant submission to the circumstances. That is weakness. Even though we may appear weak and vulnerable in a severe trial, we patiently persevere and endure it, with hope in God and an inner resilience and strength that does not give up. Indeed, where meekness is mentioned in the Bible, it usually refers to a person who is vindicated and rewarded for their patient endurance. The meek person's strong and accurate self-image enables proper self-confidence in relationships with others. It was that certainty of his identity which allowed Jesus to humble himself and wash the disciples' feet (Jn. 13:3–17). Jesus said we would be blessed if we do the same.

Meekness does not come to us naturally. Galatians 5:22 lists it as a fruit of the Spirit. Those who find the blessedness Jesus is describing here will be full of the Spirit, with his fruit manifest in our lives.

But how do we get from patient endurance to inheriting the earth? Don't meek men get trampled on and taken advantage of? Most men have been taught since childhood that to get ahead, we have to be tough and assertive. It is the arrogant who have influence in this world and seem to inherit it. But once again, Jesus turns things upside down—he will make sure that the meek inherit the earth. What is not clear is *when*. The world may laugh at our meekness, gentleness, and humility. Meanwhile, trusting in God's promise, we sit back and laugh at their attempts to control and dominate. At some point in the future, power will be taken from those who exalt themselves, and God will give dominion to the meek, to those who have submitted to him. We don't inherit the earth by our frantic striving, but through quiet trust in God. In the meantime, we are learning to live in Christ's power and reign with him in this life.

David: A meek man?

David doesn't necessarily strike us as being meek, but he wrote this in Psalm 37:5–11:

> *Commit your way to the Lord;*
> *trust in him and he will do this:*
> *He will make your righteous reward shine like the dawn,*
> *your vindication like the noonday sun.*

Be still before the Lord
and wait patiently for him;
do not fret when people succeed in their ways,
when they carry out their wicked schemes.

Refrain from anger and turn from wrath;
do not fret—it leads only to evil.
For those who are evil will be destroyed,
but those who hope in the Lord will inherit the land.

A little while, and the wicked will be no more;
though you look for them, they will not be found.
But the meek will inherit the land
and enjoy peace and prosperity.

(Psalm 37:5–11)

4

Blessed are Those who Hunger and Thirst for Righteousness

Matthew 5:6

I'm sure you have seen those horrific pictures of starving children in famine-stricken nations.

No one would say that these children are happy. Certainly not Jesus. But he draws on that image of emptiness and great need to debunk our usual understanding of happiness:

Blessed are those who hunger and thirst for righteousness, for they will be filled.

"Blessed [joyful, nourished by God's goodness] are those who hunger and thirst for righteousness [those who actively seek right standing with God], for they will be [completely] satisfied. (AMP)

We tend to think that those who pursue the wealth and pleasures of this world are the ones who are full. Their lives are exciting. They enjoy the latest technology, the fastest cars, and the most glamorous women. Surely, with their beautiful homes, great families, high positions, and practically unlimited wealth, their lives are full. Unfortunately, they are full of themselves. They often do whatever is necessary to get what they want, with no regard for what is right. They desperately try to fill an emptiness in their souls. The person who hungers for righteousness focuses on the spiritual, not the material.

Types of righteousness

- **Legal or relational righteousness,** which brings us into a right relationship with God. Through our faith in Jesus, we are justified; declared not guilty; "just-as-if-I'd" never sinned.

- **Moral righteousness**; consistently choosing to obey God and do the right thing. The Pharisees knew an external righteousness of slavishly following rules. Jesus repeatedly condemned that legalism. Unfortunately, many Christians fall into it. Our hunger must go much deeper, to the heart and will.

- **Social righteousness**. The Bible goes well beyond personal, individual righteousness. God desires to deliver us from all oppression and is interested in civil rights, a fair justice system, and integrity in the business world.

How to be filled

We are not filled based on our merits or hard work. We don't earn it by a certain number of good deeds. It is a heart attitude; a deep longing within us for God's righteousness, similar to the hunger and thirst we all experience at times. We are sick of sin, our selfishness, and the deceit of Satan and the world. The fact that we are hungering for righteousness means we have realized that our own righteousness is as filthy rags. We just don't have it within us; Jesus needs to fill us, and he promises to, by his grace.

Luke's record of Jesus' teaching adds: *What sorrow awaits you who are fat and prosperous now, for a time of awful hunger awaits you* (6:25, NTV). This offers a different perspective, implying that those who have abundance now, who are well-fed and prosperous, will face "awful hunger" in the future. This choice of having it all now (but paying for it in the future), or going without and having a more difficult life now (but receiving eternal blessings from the Lord in the future), is consistent with the other beatitudes.

- What do you hunger and thirst for? The good life? Material things? A satisfying love life? Are you willing to compromise God's word to obtain them? Have you perhaps already abandoned righteousness to pursue them?   .

- Amid all the perversion and sin in today's world, is there a desperate longing in your heart for righteousness? Almost like you are starving for holiness?

- Are you passionate about righteousness, not only in your own life, but in the world around you?

- Do you have spiritual hunger? Or has it been dulled by your involvement in the world?

Are there times when it feels like you can never achieve this righteous life? Jesus promises that you will be filled, but it is not a once-and-for-all thing, which we look back on with self-satisfaction. The idea here is of continual hungering and thirsting—just as you hunger for food and get thirsty every day. It is continually coming to Jesus to be filled.

The progression apparent in the first four beatitudes

- First, we recognize our spiritual poverty— indeed, bankruptcy—before God: There is nothing we can do to help ourselves.

- That brings us to a place of genuine mourning for our sin and brokenness, and for the hurt we have caused God and others by our sin.

- Recognizing our poverty, we assume a gentle and humble (meek) attitude toward others who are struggling, and abandon our spiritual arrogance and pride.

- Unless there is genuine change in the way we live, the first three are not worth much. There are too many "Christians" who quickly confess their poverty and need, but lack hunger for a righteous life. God promises to fill those who have a passionate desire for righteousness.

- The next three Beatitudes deal with our hearts, and how they affect our relationships with others.

Where are you at? To walk as Jesus walked, to think as Jesus thought, and to be genuinely blessed by God, we need to have this mindset. It goes against everything the world promotes and, unfortunately, what is taught in many churches as well.

5

Blessed are the Merciful

Matthew 5:7

The next three beatitudes are less controversial. They still evoke images that are more feminine than masculine, but are generally accepted as positive traits: someone who is merciful, pure in heart, and a peacemaker—qualities that affect relationships with other people. Amazingly, despite the inoffensive nature of these characteristics, the world's reaction is to persecute those who live in the kingdom culture. The beatitudes finish with the encouragement that this, too, is a blessed condition.

Do you want to be shown compassion and mercy? Walk like Jesus walked, in mercy and compassion, and you will experience them.

Blessed are the merciful, for they will be shown mercy.

What does it mean to be merciful?

Dictionary.com defines it as "compassionate or kindly forbearance shown toward an offender, an enemy, or other person in one's power; compassion, pity, or benevolence." Mercy is having a loving, tender heart, which is ready to act on behalf of anyone who needs help. You generally don't have mercy on a friend, but on someone who owes you something, who can't do anything for you, and deserves your punishment. Despite that, you choose to overlook it and bless them anyway. Mercy is closely tied to forgiveness. God expects his followers to be forgiving and merciful. He will not forgive you if you don't forgive others (Matt. 6:15). If you are unmerciful, God will not show you mercy, and others will be less likely to do so.

God desires mercy, not sacrifice

This is a fitting Beatitude to follow hungering and thirsting for righteousness. Unfortunately, it is possible to be scrupulous about personal righteousness (possibly to the point of being self-righteous), but be very unmerciful. That occasioned some of Jesus' strongest condemnation of the Pharisees:

While Jesus was having dinner at Matthew's house, many tax collectors and sinners came and ate with him and his disciples. When the Pharisees saw this, they asked his disciples, "Why does your teacher eat with tax collectors and sinners?" On hearing this, Jesus said, "It is not the healthy who need a doctor, but the sick. But go and learn what this means: 'I desire mercy, not sacrifice.' For I have not come to call the righteous, but sinners." (Matt. 9:10–13)

The Hebrew word *hesed* is often translated "lovingkindness" and includes the idea of God's covenant love, compassion, and mercy. God doesn't wait for us to ask; he takes the initiative in showing us mercy. There was nothing about Israel that merited God's miracles in delivering them from Egypt and taking them to the Promised Land. Nor can we merit or earn salvation, but God is merciful, and his mercy moves his heart to pour out love and compassion on sinners who deserve his punishment: *He saved us, not because of righteous things we had done, but because of his mercy* (Titus 3:5).

We love because he first loved us. We forgive because he forgave the much greater debt that we owed him. And we show mercy because he was merciful to us. As we grow in mercy, we become more Christ-like, share the Father's merciful heart, and experience the godly character he desires to develop in us. Later, in the same sermon, Jesus summed up this teaching with the "Golden rule:" *So in everything, do to others what you would have them do to you, for this sums up the Law and the Prophets* (Matt. 7:12).

The parable of the unmerciful servant (Matthew 18)

Mercy is often expressed in acts of charity. The parable of the Good Samaritan (Lk. 10:25–37) is a stunning judgment on unmerciful religious leaders, and a lesson in the lengths to which true mercy goes in helping others. It shows the pro-active nature of mercy, taking advantage of every opportunity to be compassionate. Another parable, of the unmerciful servant, vividly portrays the consequences of being unmerciful and demonstrates the mercy that spares us from our deserved punishment:

²¹ *Then Peter came to Jesus and asked, "Lord, how many times shall I forgive my brother or sister who sins against me? Up to seven times?"*

²² *Jesus answered, "I tell you, not seven times, but seventy-seven times.*

Limits cannot be placed on our forgiveness of others or their response to it, nor on the mercy shown to others. What stops the flow of forgiveness or mercy is an unforgiving or unmerciful response on the part of the one receiving mercy.

²³ *"Therefore, the kingdom of heaven is like a king who wanted to settle accounts with his servants. ²⁴ As he began the settlement, a man who owed him ten thousand bags of gold was brought to him. ²⁵ Since he was not able to pay, the master ordered that he and his wife and his children and all that he had be sold to repay the debt.*

The debt we owe God is impossible to pay, but he has every right to demand repayment.

²⁶ *"At this the servant fell on his knees before him. 'Be patient with me,' he begged, 'and I will pay back everything.' ²⁷ The servant's master took pity on him, canceled the debt and let him go.*

In this case (as opposed to the Samaritan), the master waited to be asked. Then his merciful heart moved him to have compassion, take pity on the servant, and let him go.

²⁸ "But when that servant went out, he found one of his fellow servants who owed him a hundred silver coins. He grabbed him and began to choke him. 'Pay back what you owe me!' he demanded.

²⁹ "His fellow servant fell to his knees and begged him, 'Be patient with me, and I will pay it back.'

³⁰ "But he refused. Instead, he went off and had the man thrown into prison until he could pay the debt. ³¹ When the other servants saw what had happened, they were outraged and went and told their master everything that had happened.

The other servants, observing the mercy shown the first servant, expected the same, and beg for it. But the first servant refuses:

³² "Then the master called the servant in. 'You wicked servant,' he said, 'I canceled all that debt of yours because you begged me to. ³³ Shouldn't you have had mercy on your fellow servant just as I had on you?' ³⁴ In anger his master handed him over to the jailers to be tortured, until he should pay back all he owed.

³⁵ "This is how my heavenly Father will treat each of you unless you forgive your brother or sister from your heart."

The close connection between forgiveness and mercy is shown here: God expects us to have mercy on others who are clearly undeserving, just as he has had mercy on us. As he sees your tender, compassionate, and merciful heart, not only will you experience *his* mercy, but he will also incline *others* to be merciful to you.

Lack of mercy affects your salvation

One of Jesus' last teachings emphasizes the importance of mercy and shows an intriguing, definitive link between righteousness and mercy:

"Then the King will say to those on his right, 'Come, you who are blessed by my Father; take your inheritance, the kingdom prepared for you since the creation of the world.[35] *For I was hungry and you gave me something to eat, I was thirsty and you gave me something to drink, I was a stranger and you invited me in,* [36] *I needed clothes and you clothed me, I was sick and you looked after me, I was in prison and you came to visit me.'*

[37] *"Then the righteous will answer him, 'Lord, when did we see you hungry and feed you, or thirsty and give you something to drink?* [38] *When did we see you a stranger and invite you in, or needing clothes and clothe you?* [39] *When did we see you sick or in prison and go to visit you?'*

[40] *"The King will reply, 'Truly I tell you, whatever you did for one of the least of these brothers and sisters of mine, you did for me.'* (Matt. 25:34–40)

Those who failed to show mercy are cast into hell. Yes, mercy is a salvation issue. Jesus expects us to look for opportunities to be merciful and show mercy to the very least, to those who can never repay us.

- In what ways has God shown you mercy? Have you even been aware of it? Have you thanked him for it?

- Do you need to ask him for mercy?

- Are there opportunities for you to show compassion, forgiveness, and mercy to someone who clearly does not deserve it?

- Do you risk having to repay your debt to God, or even be cast into hell, because you failed to be merciful?

If you are a merciful person, be assured that God will show you mercy in your time of need. Don't hesitate to ask him for it. The nature of mercy means that, even with our imperfections, God continues showing us mercy, and for that, we genuinely need to be grateful.

It is not easy to be merciful and compassionate in today's world. There are too many cases of someone taking a stranger into their home, only to have him rape their daughter or rob them. You need much discernment and guidance from the Holy Spirit. But when God gives you the opportunity to be compassionate to someone, you must walk like Jesus walked and show them mercy.

6

Blessed are the Pure in Heart

Matthew 5:8

Holiness is not just following rules, like abstaining from smoking, drinking, and sexual sin. Holiness goes much deeper:

⁸ Blessed are the pure in heart, for they will see God.

"Blessed [anticipating God's presence, spiritually mature] are the pure in heart [those with integrity, moral courage, and godly character], for they will see God. (AMP)

Jesus is about to apply this to anger and lust:

"You have heard that it was said to the people long ago, 'You shall not murder, and anyone who murders will be subject to judgment.' But I tell you that anyone angry with a brother or sister will be subject to judgment (Matt. 5:21–22).

"You have heard that it was said, 'You shall not commit adultery.' But I tell you that anyone who looks at a

woman lustfully has already committed adultery with her in his heart (Matt. 5:27–28).

Under the law, the emphasis was on the externals. Your heart could be full of murderous, adulterous thoughts, but as long as no one died or you never touched another woman, you were fine. Jesus says, "Not really."

"Woe to you, teachers of the law and Pharisees, you hypocrites! You clean the outside of the cup and dish, but inside they are full of greed and self-indulgence. Blind Pharisee! First, clean the inside of the cup and dish, and then the outside will also be clean." (Matt. 23:25–26)

God is interested in the heart. If your heart is pure, your actions and thoughts will reflect it; if your heart is filthy, sooner or later it will show up in the way you live. In Matthew 6, Jesus goes on to talk about the importance of offerings, prayers, and fasting coming from the heart. If it is for external show, to impress others, it is of little benefit. You might maintain a legalistic appearance of purity, but you won't see God or enjoy a relationship with him: *Make every effort to live in peace with everyone and to be holy; without holiness no one will see the Lord* (Hebrews 12:14).

The importance of heart purity was not a new concept for the Jews. The Holy Spirit had given David the same thought in Psalm 73:1:

Surely God is good to Israel, to those who are pure in heart.

David expanded on the same idea in Psalm 24:3–6:

Who may ascend the mountain of the Lord?
Who may stand in his holy place?
The one who has clean hands and a pure heart,
who does not trust in an idol
or swear by a false god.

They will receive blessing from the Lord
and vindication from God their Savior.
Such is the generation of those who seek him,
who seek your face, God of Jacob.

These believers *sought* God's face, but were unable to see it, even though David said in Psalm 17:15: *And I – in righteousness I will see your face; when I awake, I will be satisfied with seeing your likeness.*

How do you reconcile that with God's oft-repeated words to Moses in Exodus 33:20: *But," he said, "you cannot see my face, for no one may see me and live."* Jesus takes the possibility for intimacy with God to a new level, just as he does with our understanding of a life that pleases God. It is possible to see God, but only for the pure in heart, and most likely it will be in heaven: *They will see his face, and his name will be on their foreheads...And they will reign for ever and ever* (Rev. 22:4–5).

How is your heart? You might put on a good show in church and in front of your family, but what happens when you are with your friends? When you see a beautiful woman on the street? When you are tempted by porn on the internet? Your whole life—public and private, thoughts and motivations—should be transparent before God and others. Many people think "purity of heart" is boring. They find their thrills in anything but purity. But they are deceived. Jesus said the truly blessed person is the one who can see God, and that is only possible with a pure heart. That is where real happiness is found.

If you feel like you have lost your connection with God, like you no longer see him, check the purity of your heart. Hopefully, you have known times when God mercifully cleans out the darkest corners of your heart, and you feel incredibly clean. He may need to do some heart cleaning for you today. He wants to. He wants you to see his face, but he can't tolerate a filthy heart. Let the blood of Jesus cleanse you.

Several more times, Jesus says, "You have heard that it was said," but the final one is an excellent lead-in to the rest of the Beatitudes:

"You have heard that it was said, 'Love your neighbor and hate your enemy.' But I tell you, love your enemies and pray for those who persecute you (Matt. 5:43–44).

7

Blessed are the Peacemakers

Matthew 5:9

⁹ Blessed are the peacemakers, for they will be called children of God.

My mother was the peacemaker in our family. She hated conflict. My father could have a volatile temper, but she would always step in to calm things down, and he would head to the basement to deal with his anger. I learned to avoid conflict at all costs: do whatever is necessary to keep the peace, even if it means bottling up the anger. That's not healthy. Conflict avoidance is not peacemaking. Making peace can be costly—just ask Jesus. He made peace between God and humanity, satisfying the Father's wrath, at the price of his own life.

It makes sense that the Prince of Peace would bless the peacemakers! *For God was pleased to have all his fullness dwell in him, and through him to reconcile to himself all things, whether things on earth or things in heaven, by making peace through his blood, shed on the cross* (Col. 3:19–20).

Have you known people who seem to create conflict wherever they go? The root is often pride or insecurity. Those who are pure in heart tend to create less conflict; their very presence brings peace to a troubled situation. James (3:17–18) spoke of that heavenly wisdom:

But the wisdom that comes from heaven is first of all pure; then peace-loving, considerate, submissive, full of mercy and good fruit, impartial and sincere. Peacemakers who sow in peace reap a harvest of righteousness.

Romans 14 offers some wise counsel on keeping peace in the church, especially verse 19: *Let us therefore make every effort to do what leads to peace and to mutual edification.*

If we focus on mutual edification, we will foster peace. Peacemaking can involve considerable effort; don't be lazy! Be careful in any situation (work, school, church, home) not to jump into a conflict, take sides, and make it worse. Try to be objective and see all sides of an issue. Meekness, as we studied it here, also lends itself to peacemaking. Ask God to give you wisdom on how to resolve the conflict. Don't impose a solution, but listen carefully, affirm the feelings of those involved, and speak with authority when necessary. Be aware that peace will not always be possible. That grieves the Father's heart, and it grieves us to live with conflict in the home or on the job. You can pray and do your part, and entrust the results to God. Pray for peace in the world, and do whatever you can to promote peace in your community. Pray for ways your church can be involved in peacemaking.

God wants to use you as an agent of healing in the world around you. The earlier Beatitudes give us the foundation; make sure your heart is pure, and walk in mercy, bringing peace and God's presence. Unfortunately, as we will see in the final Beatitudes, the world often rejects that presence.

8

Blessed are the Persecuted

Matthew 5:10-12

J esus opened his sermon with a description of the "blessed life." Unfortunately, it bears little resemblance to what is regularly promoted in today's church. Poor? Meek? Hungry? Pure in heart? Is Jesus trying to discourage us from following him? It seems like it, especially with this shocking conclusion to his beatitudes:

10 Blessed are those who are persecuted because of righteousness, for theirs is the kingdom of heaven.

God blesses those who are persecuted for doing right, for the Kingdom of Heaven is theirs. (NLT)

He just said we should be known as peacemakers! Indeed, that should be our aim, but it may not be possible in a fallen world. Few people welcome persecution, but it isn't all bad! In fact, if we never experience it, we may have to question if we are truly following Jesus.

43

God's heart is moved when we suffer for following him and doing what is right. He pours out his blessings on us! There is something about persecution that enables us to understand what the kingdom of heaven is and enter into it. Those who enjoy the world's acclaim and never know suffering or persecution are often so comfortable in this world that it may be hard for them to embrace God's kingdom. Remember Jesus' words in Luke 6:26:

Woe to you when everyone speaks well of you,
   for that is how their ancestors treated the false
prophets.

Somehow, many Christians in the United States think the constitution protects them from persecution, which they associate with communism or Muslim extremism. But increasingly, at the first sign of any opposition, they cry "persecution!" and fear they are losing their religious freedom.

What qualifies as persecution?

Unfortunately, not everyone who suffers is doing what is right! There is no blessing if you are being unloving or an all-around jerk!

For it is commendable if someone bears up under the pain of unjust suffering because they are conscious of God. But how is it to your credit if you receive a beating for doing wrong and endure it? But if you suffer for doing good and you endure it, this is commendable before God. To this you were called, because Christ suffered for you, leaving you an example, that you should follow in his steps. "He committed no sin, and no deceit was found in his mouth." When they hurled their insults at him, he did not retaliate; when he suffered, he made no threats. Instead, he entrusted himself to him who judges justly (1 Pet. 2:19–23).

Peter witnessed Christ's suffering firsthand and had already suffered for his faith. He is well qualified to speak about persecution:

- Christ was misunderstood, rejected, persecuted, and eventually crucified. We are called to follow his example.

- Suffering does not necessarily mean you are in sin. Strong faith and obedience to God do not guarantee a pain-free life!

- It is especially hard to bear unmerited suffering. We want to cry out for justice! But we are called to endure it.

- We must resist the urge to retaliate and insult those who insult us.

- Do not threaten hell or God's judgment on those who are persecuting you. Let God deal with them.

- Even if it means death, we trust God to take care of us. That faith and confidence enable us to see beyond the current suffering.

God's purpose in suffering

God uses suffering, even in the life of his own Son:

Son though he was, he learned obedience from what he suffered and, once made perfect, he became the source of eternal salvation for all who obey him (Heb. 5:8–9).

If Jesus benefited from suffering, we can expect to as well. How is your obedience to Christ? Could God be allowing your suffering now to help you grow in obedience? Does God need to allow more, to perfect that obedience? Is God calling you to make costly decisions?

The last two verses of the Beatitudes

Jesus' teaching on persecution is consistent with many of his other teachings: live a comfortable life now, but pay for it in eternity, or suffer now, and reap eternal rewards. The final verses of the Beatitudes promise blessings and abundant heavenly rewards for those who are persecuted because of their faith:

[11] *"Blessed are you when people insult you, persecute you and falsely say all kinds of evil against you because of me.* [12] *Rejoice and be glad, because great is your reward in heaven, for in the same way they persecuted the prophets who were before you.*

"God blesses you when people mock you and persecute you and lie about you and say all sorts of evil things against you because you are my followers. Be happy about it! Be very glad! For a great reward awaits you in heaven. And remember, the ancient prophets were persecuted in the same way. (NLT)

- To qualify as persecution, it must be a result of your identification with Jesus, being recognized as his follower, and doing what is right. Persecution because of your foolishness doesn't count.

- You can expect to be mocked, insulted, and have all kinds of evil things (probably lies or half-truths) spoken about you.

- You should not only bear the persecution, but rejoice and be glad in it, because others see Jesus in you and target you with their hatred for him.

- You are receiving the same treatment that faithful men and women of God have experienced through the ages. It is not unusual, and you are not being singled out.

After the suffering

Remember those earlier days after you had received the light, when you endured in a great conflict full of suffering. Sometimes you were publicly exposed to insult and persecution; at other times you stood side by side with those who were so treated. You suffered along with those in prison and joyfully accepted the confiscation of your property, because you knew that you yourselves had better and lasting possessions. So do not throw away your confidence; it will be richly rewarded (Heb. 10:32–35).

The persecuted church tends to produce strong believers. In many countries, when persecution finally ends, the church becomes complacent and loses its former strength. The believers receiving the letter to the

Hebrews had known severe persecution. Now, after a period of peace, they are suffering again and struggling to maintain their faith.

- A rich reward awaits those who persevere and endure the persecution.

- Part of the earlier persecution included the confiscation of their personal property. Instead of lamenting it and fighting for their rights, they had joyfully accepted it, mindful that our worldly possessions pale in comparison with the lasting possessions awaiting us in heaven. Persecution helps us focus on eternity!

- The insults and persecution are often public, for all the world to see.

- If you have been graced to escape persecution, you are called to stand side by side with those who are suffering. There are many opportunities to do that today, with the unprecedented amount of persecution. Groups like Voice of the Martyrs enable you to stand with the persecuted church.

- There may be times when you are called to identify with those who are suffering. In this case, it probably included visiting those in prison for their faith, and possibly even doing time with them!

The experience of heroes of the faith

Do you think great faith will keep you from suffering, or that suffering is somehow a sign of weak faith? Do you think you have it rough? This is the experience of many of the great heroes of the faith:

Some faced jeers and flogging, and even chains and imprisonment. They were put to death by stoning; they were sawed in two; they were killed by the sword. They went about in sheepskins and goatskins, destitute, persecuted and mistreated— the world was not worthy of them. They wandered in deserts and mountains, living in caves and in holes in the ground (Heb. 11:36–38).

We really don't have it that bad. Pray for those who are persecuted and dying for their faith!

God's promise and provision in suffering

If your life is currently trouble-free, praise God! You don't need to adopt a martyr's complex or try to provoke persecution so you can somehow reap more blessings. But don't get complacent. Especially with the current world situation, we can expect persecution to increase. Are you prepared? Will you be able to endure and even rejoice in the suffering?

The testimony of countless persecuted believers is that they experience God's love like never before in the midst of their suffering. Not only can you be confident that nothing will separate you from Christ's love; he has promised that you are more than a conqueror in every situation!

Who shall separate us from the love of Christ?

Shall trouble or hardship or persecution or famine or nakedness or danger or sword?

As it is written:

"For your sake we face death all day long; we are considered as sheep to be slaughtered."

No, in all these things we are more than conquerors through him who loved us.

(Romans 8:35-37)

9

The Nature of the Kingdom

Matthew 18:1–20

Matthew 18 is the fourth of Jesus' five discourses in this Gospel (the first is the Sermon on the Mount; the last is chapter 24, about the end of the world and Jesus' return). The Beatitudes have given us an introduction to kingdom culture; this teaching applies it to our relationships.

Who is the most important?

The chapter opens with the disciples posing this question to Jesus:

¹*"Who, then, is the greatest in the kingdom of heaven?"*

I'm sure they weren't expecting his answer:

²*He called a little child to him, and placed the child among them. ³And he said: "Truly I tell you, unless you change and become like little children, you will never enter the kingdom of heaven. ⁴Therefore, whoever takes the lowly position of this child is the greatest in the*

kingdom of heaven. ⁵ And whoever welcomes one such child in my name welcomes me.

It's not about being *great* in the kingdom, but about *entering* the kingdom. They were still in the world, thinking about position, power, and material rewards. From the world's perspective, everything in the kingdom is backward. To enter the kingdom (to be saved), we must forsake the world's way of thinking, change (repent), and become like a little child. Obviously, that is not physically possible, just as we can't go back to our mother's womb to be born again. But spiritually, we must humble ourselves and start all over again, as a baby, with the humility, simplicity, and heart of a child. It is easy to get caught up in competing for position in the church, organizing it, and making it a business. It is harder to become like a child, weak and dependent, without position or influence.

In addition, Jesus says there is a special blessing for those who welcome (or receive) a child in his name, as he said in Mark 9:41: *If anyone gives you even a cup of water because you belong to the Messiah, I tell you the truth, that person will surely be rewarded.* Or in Matthew 25:40, where Jesus spoke of ministering to the neediest: *"And the King will say, 'I tell you the truth, when you did it to one of the least of these my brothers and sisters, you were doing it to me!'* Part of humbling ourselves like a child is receiving other "children" with open arms; the ones rejected by the world should find a warm welcome in the church.

- Have you entered the kingdom?

- Have you changed and become humble like a child?

- Do you welcome children? Or are you still caught up with the world's mentality, seeking fame, position, power, and wealth?

The seriousness of sin

[6] "If anyone causes one of these little ones—those who believe in me—to stumble, it would be better for them to have a large millstone hung around their neck and to be drowned in the depths of the sea. [7] Woe to the world because of the things that cause people to stumble! Such things must come, but woe to the person through whom they come! [8] If your hand or your foot causes you to stumble, cut it off and throw it away. It is better for you to enter life maimed or crippled than to have two hands or two feet and be thrown into eternal fire. [9] And if your eye causes you to stumble, gouge it out and throw it away. It is better for you to enter life with one eye than to have two eyes and be thrown into the fire of hell.

To cause someone to stumble or sin, especially a child, or someone with the humility and faith of a child, is very serious. A child naturally trusts others, and betrayal by a pastor, parent, or someone they trust can be devastating. Unfortunately, in this world, there are evil people who will cause others to sin, but they will be severely judged. We must do everything possible to avoid sin and not make a little one stumble.

Jesus gave two extreme examples to illustrate the severity of sin and the need to fight it ruthlessly.

Obviously, he doesn't expect us to tie a rock around the sinner's neck and throw him into the sea to drown. Nor does he expect us to mutilate ourselves. The church would be full of blind cripples! There are stories of men in the past who cut off their genitals to avoid sin. Jesus does not want that!

To say "he made me sin" is no excuse for sin. The one who habitually practices sin cannot enter the kingdom; he has not repented and does not have the heart or simplicity of a child. Sin is so dangerous—it can get you thrown into the fire of hell!—that we must do whatever is necessary to overcome it.

- Are you a stumbling block to some child, or someone who is child-like?

- Is there someone who caused you to sin in the past that you need to forgive? Have you accepted your responsibility for the sin (if there was any), or do you just blame him?

- Are you doing everything possible to avoid sin? If you have to cut off the internet to avoid pornography, are you ready to go to that extreme?

The importance of each "little one"

[10] *"See that you do not despise one of these little ones. For I tell you that their angels in heaven always see the face of my Father in heaven.*

Jesus just said that a child is the greatest in the kingdom, but we tend to look down on children instead of lifting them up. "Despise" is a strong word which means "to regard with contempt, distaste, disgust, or disdain; scorn; loathe" (*dictionary.com*). You don't have to make someone stumble to be guilty of this sin. Why is it so serious?

Jesus introduces the well-known concept of a "guardian angel." Apparently, everyone has an angel who dwells in God's presence, but a child's angel has the privilege of always seeing God's face. If their angels have that privilege, we certainly should honor the children in our midst.

12 "What do you think? If a man owns a hundred sheep, and one of them wanders away, will he not leave the ninety-nine on the hills and go to look for the one that wandered off? 13 And if he finds it, truly I tell you, he is happier about that one sheep than about the ninety-nine that did not wander off. 14 In the same way your Father in heaven is not willing that any of these little ones should perish.

In the kingdom, everyone has infinite value. God will do everything possible to seek and find a wandering sheep. There is special joy in the return of a backslidden sinner who repents and returns to the Lord. It reminds us of the parable of the prodigal son: the father's joy when his son returns home, and the older brother's jealousy (Lk. 15:11–31). Here, the lost sheep is a "little one." They may be more apt to wander, but the Father's heart is very tender toward them. He is determined not to lose any of his children.

The Bible gives us great promises for our prayers. Verse 14 clearly says it is not God's will that any little one would perish. Peter said the same in 2 Peter 3:9: *He is patient with you, not wanting anyone to perish, but everyone to come to repentance.* If you are praying for your backslidden spouse or child, hold onto this word. The person who seeks wandering sheep and cares for the little ones will find a special blessing and help from the Father. Likewise, the man who causes one of those sheep to wander will be judged severely.

- Is there a "lost sheep" in your church you need to go looking for? In your family?

- Have you been guilty of writing off a backslidden brother or gossiping about him?

- Do you need to pray with renewed faith for a wandering spouse or child, confident that God does not want them to perish?

The brother who sins against you

[15] *"If your brother or sister sins, go and point out their fault, just between the two of you. If they listen to you, you have won them over.*[16] *But if they will not listen, take one or two others along, so that 'every matter may be established by the testimony of two or three witnesses.'*[17] *If they still refuse to listen, tell it to the church; and if they refuse to listen even to the church, treat them as you would a pagan or a tax collector.*

Some versions say the brother "sins against you," others just say "sins." Either way, the Body of Christ must be kept clean and sin-free, and every member is responsible for their part. In the kingdom, there is no room for resentment, hatred, revenge, or gossip. Jesus gives us a straightforward procedure to follow:

1. It may be difficult, but talk to the person alone, praying that the Holy Spirit would reveal their sin. You might be mistaken, and they didn't even do anything wrong.

2. If they don't receive you and ask you and God for forgiveness, go back with one or two others (often a pastor, elder, or mature believer), not to gang up on them, but in love to seek a resolution to the problem.

3. If they still don't respond, bring the situation before the church, not to condemn them, but to pray for them and help them. Jesus doesn't say exactly how that would be done.

4. If they refuse to repent, they should no longer be considered a brother or sister in Christ.

Church discipline is a very delicate topic and requires much prayer and the anointing of the Spirit. If done in the flesh, it can cause great harm to a person and perhaps alienate them from Christ for good. We must also balance what Jesus just said about seeking the lost sheep (18:12) with treating them as an unbeliever and rejecting them as a brother or sister. The Father's heart (which should be ours as well) is always for the person's restoration. We keep praying and doing all we can toward that end.

Next is a powerful tool that God has given us for that battle.

Power and authority in the Kingdom

[18] "Truly I tell you, whatever you bind on earth will be bound in heaven, and whatever you loose on earth will be loosed in heaven. [19] "Again, truly I tell you that if two of you on earth agree about anything they ask for, it will be done for them by my Father in heaven. [20] For where two or three gather in my name, there am I with them."

We have seen the need for humility, reconciliation, and purity in the church. We cannot tolerate sin; it separates us from God and other believers. But Jesus knows that sometimes, despite all our efforts:

- There will still be stumbling blocks in the church.

- There will be sins that we seem unable to overcome.

- There will be wandering sheep who don't want to come back to the flock.

- Some will be offended by church discipline and refuse to repent. They may fall into grievous sin or cause divisions in the church.

The temptation for many churches is to reject the person, gossip about them, and talk about how they hung out with the wrong crowd or were inconsistent with their tithe or church attendance. Jesus gives us another option: God himself shares his authority and power with us.

Traditionally, the church has taught that binding and loosing applied to offering or withholding forgiveness to the sinner. But Jesus says *"whatever,"* and makes no condition. In the kingdom, we have the authority to bind that evil spirit that leads someone to cause others to sin. We bind those addictions that keep them bound in drugs or pornography. We bind the blindness that keeps them from seeing their fault, and robs them of clear vision, and we loose forgiveness, mercy, humility, and God's power.

That same authority to bind and loose was given to Peter when he confessed Jesus as the Messiah:

Simon Peter answered, "You are the Messiah, the Son of the living God."

Jesus replied, "Blessed are you, Simon son of Jonah, for this was not revealed to you by flesh and blood, but by my Father in heaven. And I tell you that you are Peter, and on this rock I will build my church, and the gates of Hades will not overcome it. I will give you the keys of the kingdom of heaven; whatever you bind on earth will be bound in heaven, and whatever you loose on earth will be loosed in heaven" (Matt. 16:16–19).

Some have mistakenly thought that Jesus gave Peter a unique authority as the first "pope." But here, in chapter 18, Jesus gives this same authority to every believer. The "rock" of the church is the faith that Jesus is the Son of God. This authority is exercised in the context of the church and the healthy relationships we have studied in this chapter. The kingdom of God is a kingdom of power! He also gives us an amazing promise that empowers us to set things in order in the church: if two believers agree on anything they ask, the Father will do it. It is a blank check: *"anything."* And there is no condition given: *"it will be done for them."* We do have to be in agreement, which is why unity and reconciliation between believers are so essential. We are not talking about a superficial agreement, but having the same heart, and agreement in the Spirit.

Jesus himself is present when two or three are gathered in his name. The church is not a game, a social club, or a business. It is Christ's Body, the expression of God's kingdom here on earth. Every member possesses great value, power, and authority.

I was also a sinner! God saved me! I must be patient, compassionate, and merciful to sinners. Forgiving them is not optional. If I don't forgive my brother *from the heart*, God will not forgive me, and I will be tortured in the eternal fires of hell.

If little ones are mistreated, if there is sin and lack of unity, Christ will not be present, there will be no authority to bind and loose, and no answered prayer. This whole chapter is a call to humble ourselves, acknowledge God's mercy in our lives, and offer the same compassion and forgiveness to others. That humility and unity touch the Father's heart and release his power on our behalf.

10

Dinner with Jesus

Luke 14:1–24

J esus was the special guest at this dinner. In the span of a few hours, he manages to heal someone, give profound teaching (probably much deeper than they had heard in synagogue that morning), and challenge some of the most important people in that town. In the process, he teaches us much about the culture of his kingdom. What an example for us to follow! Make the most of every opportunity at dinner–or anytime!

¹One Sabbath, when Jesus went to eat in the house of a prominent Pharisee, he was being carefully watched. ² There in front of him was a man suffering from abnormal swelling of his body.

The situation

- It was the Sabbath, the day of rest, a day to worship God and fellowship with other believers.

- Old Testament law prohibited work on that day, but over the years, rabbis had added many rules, making the day more of a duty than a blessing.

- Sometimes Jesus taught in the synagogue on the Sabbath. We don't know if he did that week or not.

- The synagogue service probably had finished, and a sizable group moved to this home for dinner.

Have you noticed that Jesus liked to eat? We frequently find him at meals! Just before his arrest, he shared one Last Supper with his disciples. One of his last acts on earth was preparing breakfast for them. And we are looking forward to the wedding banquet of the Lamb. The food will be amazing!

Jesus didn't have his own house. He had no kitchen and no wife to prepare meals, but God always provided the food he needed! We never saw him in a restaurant, but he received many invitations to dine in homes, and we never saw him refuse an invitation. Shared meals are important, whether in your own home or as a guest.

Jesus was comfortable in mansions—and the most humble home. This must have been a very nice house. It appears there were a lot of people there, and important people. This Pharisee was a leader in the community. Things often were tense between Jesus and the Pharisees, but that didn't stop him from going to his home. If Jesus were invited to someone's home—even when he knew they had mixed motives—he would gladly go. He trusted his Father to be his "social secretary," and expected that there was a purpose in him being there. When we go with that attitude, we can expect God to give us opportunities to minister.

They watched him carefully

Do you know what it is like to have people watching you? Maybe people from another country, culture, or social class. Or your boss, or pastor. They're not watching you with admiration, but as a curiosity, or with the hopes of catching you doing something wrong. It can make you feel like an animal in the zoo!

The people at this dinner party were watching Jesus' every move. The Amplified Bible says: *they were watching Him closely and carefully [hoping to entrap Him]*. This was a setup. Jesus knew it. It wasn't the first time, and he didn't care. He could handle it.

How do you respond to a setup? Do you get angry? Start a fight? Get out of there? Or do you ask God to give you wisdom, and to use the situation for his purposes?

Do you watch Jesus carefully? Not to trap him, but studying how he works in other people, in the church, and in your own life? Do you study him carefully in the Gospels?

In this picture-perfect home, there was just one person out of place, but he was in a good place: in front of Jesus. The man was obviously sick. Older versions say dropsy. We're not sure of the exact disease, although Luke would know, since he was a doctor. It may have been an extreme and grotesque swelling of the arms and legs. Jews considered it a sign of uncleanness and immorality, so this man probably wasn't part of this circle of prominent people. He didn't have the resources to seek medical treatment, and Jesus sent him away after he was healed, probably to go and share the good news with his family. Most likely, the Pharisees had looked for someone sick whom they could use to test Jesus. Would he heal on the Sabbath? There are seven recorded incidents when he did; it was one of the most controversial parts of his ministry, but Jesus was never one to avoid controversy.

How do you handle a setup?

You could feel the tension. All these very proper, very religious leaders. A grotesquely sick man. And Jesus. What will he do? The silence was deafening.

Don't be afraid of the test or an awkward situation. God will give you wisdom. Stand firm on your convictions. Trust in the Lord. If you are in his will, he will help you.

³ Jesus asked the Pharisees and experts in the law, "Is it lawful to heal on the Sabbath or not?" ⁴ But they remained silent. So taking hold of the man, he healed him and sent him on his way.

Jesus was well aware of what was in their hearts. He had his own setup for them. Jesus was an expert at using questions. It is better to make someone think and force them to answer a question than to attack them. Let them condemn themselves. The Lord will give you wisdom to ask questions that force them to provide the answer you want.

The Pharisees were between a rock and a hard place:

- If they say it is unlawful, they have no scriptural support from Old Testament law, and they will look cruel.

- If they say it is lawful, they will violate their own rules and will have to concede defeat.

They couldn't answer, so they stayed silent. (Men can be good at doing that with their wives.)

Jesus took hold of the man. Probably no one would want to touch him, but I picture Jesus giving him a big embrace. Instantly, he was healed. It is hard to argue with a miracle. It looks like Jesus didn't have to say anything. We need fewer words and more power. More manifestations of the Spirit. More healings and deliverances. It's like the blind man Jesus healed. His parents said, "*All we know is he was blind, and now he can see.*" They couldn't make a case against Jesus. There are still people today who believe Jesus no longer heals or does miracles, but it's hard to make their case when a miracle happens right in front of them.

They intended to trap Jesus and possibly put a decisive end to this threatening ministry. In that situation, some would point out their hypocrisy and hard hearts, but not Jesus. He had a lot more to tell them. He didn't want to lose them yet. He may know there were some there who had ears to hear. He just asked another question:

⁵ Then he asked them, "If one of you has a child or an ox that falls into a well on the Sabbath day, will you not immediately pull it out?" ⁶ And they had nothing to say.

Jesus was very familiar with Jewish practice. He knew they would save an ox that fell in a well on the Sabbath, but they would not allow for the healing of a sick man. If we are going to confront hypocrisy in the church and society, we have to know what they believe and practice, and then learn from Jesus how to confront the hypocrisy—coming across as holier than thou is usually not the most effective approach. Once again, Jesus chose to use a question he knew they couldn't answer.

We don't know how long the silence lasted. Maybe a servant finally came from the kitchen to announce that dinner was ready. Everyone scrambled for seats. Nothing has changed in 2000 years. There are always people who want to be at the front of the buffet line or in the best seats. Next to the pastor. But instead of seating Jesus as an honored guest, apparently they left him to find his seat. He waited until everyone else was seated, because he had another lesson to teach.

How to avoid embarrassment

⁷ When he noticed how the guests picked the places of honor at the table, he told them this parable:

The Pharisees were not the only ones watching what was going on. Jesus was observing everything, and what he saw was very normal. We naturally go for the first place. Nobody wants to be last. We want the best seats, and we want to be sure we get to the buffet line in time to get our favorite foods. Jesus seized the opportunity to expose their hearts – but once again, he did it with class. He used a parable and the example of a wedding. It could appear that Jesus simply wanted to save them from embarrassment. He said something that is common sense, but which we often ignore in our quest to be first.

8 "When someone invites you to a wedding feast, do not take the place of honor, for a person more distinguished than you may have been invited. 9 If so, the host who invited both of you will come and say to you, 'Give this person your seat.' Then, humiliated, you will have to take the least important place.

Learn from Jesus how to use parables and communicate the truth without alienating people. Jesus didn't condemn them as being self-seeking or self-exalting. He allowed their conscience to convict them. They were not deaf or stupid. They could get the message.

10 But when you are invited, take the lowest place, so that when your host comes, he will say to you, 'Friend, move up to a better place.' Then you will be honored in the presence of all the other guests.

There is nothing wrong with being honored in the presence of others! What is wrong is manipulating things yourself to be honored. Make it a practice in every situation to take the lowest place. Wait for the other person to tell you to move up. And if they don't, rejoice in your humble position.

This was a lesson the Pharisees should have known. Jesus was probably citing Proverbs 25:6–7:

> *Do not exalt yourself in the king's presence,*
> *and do not claim a place among his great men;*
> *it is better for him to say to you, "Come up here,"*
> *than for him to humiliate you before his nobles.*

If you are in a position to honor someone by offering them a better position (if they deserve it), by all means do! You can bless and encourage them! But don't fall into the trap of doing it for political advantage or your own benefit.

Those who humble themselves will be exalted

11 For all those who exalt themselves will be humbled, and those who humble themselves will be exalted."

Here is a universal truth. Jesus was sharing God's heart. Many at that dinner may have been convicted of their lack of humility. Jesus had their attention. They had a new respect for him. They were impressed by the way he communicated the truth.

In your teaching and study of the Word, always look for that key point, something that people will remember. It has a bigger impact when you are in the midst of a real-life situation, like this meal. People sitting in church for a half-hour (or an hour and a half) sermon have a much harder time remembering the message.

Trust in God. Humble yourself. Trust that in his time, God will lift you up. Be careful not to exalt yourself at home, church, or work. Humility is at the heart of kingdom culture.

This practical teaching, which everyone could relate to in daily life, opened the door for Jesus to share deeper spiritual truth.

Advice for a successful supper

[12] Then Jesus said to his host, "When you give a luncheon or dinner, do not invite your friends, your brothers or sisters, your relatives, or your rich neighbors; if you do, they may invite you back and so you will be repaid.

Jesus turned to his host. He knew that all the guests (except himself and the man he healed) were friends, family, or community leaders. The man probably had several motives for inviting them:

- To allow them to get to know this controversial new rabbi.
- To be the first in the town to invite Jesus to his house.
- To impress Jesus with his importance in the community.

Jesus challenged the usual reasons for giving a dinner party:

- Examine your motives in giving the meal.
- Don't always invite the same people.
- Don't do it so you can be repaid and recognized.
- Don't invite your friends, family, or rich neighbors.

[13] But when you give a banquet, invite the poor, the crippled, the lame, the blind, [14] and you will be blessed. Although they cannot repay you, you will be repaid at the resurrection of the righteous."

When I was growing up, my mother carefully noted whom she invited to our house, and if they invited us to their home. If they didn't return the invitation, they weren't invited back. That is very common. Many churches even teach that we give offerings so we can receive back more in return. But Jesus said it is more important to be repaid in the future, at the resurrection (which, incidentally, he affirmed will happen!). He implied that if we get repaid now, that may be the only reward we get.

A whole new way of viewing hospitality

- Bless those who can't repay you.
- Invite people no one else wants in their homes.
- Don't just prepare a dinner for them—prepare a banquet!

It is not a sin to invite your friends to dinner, but move out of your comfort zone. Who are the poor, crippled, lame, and blind you can invite to your house? Jesus says *when* you give a banquet, not *if* you do. Hospitality is an important part of being a Christian. How might it impact your church and community if all the Christians put this simple advice into practice?

15 When one of those who were reclining at the table with Him heard this, he said to Him, "Blessed is everyone who will eat bread in the kingdom of God!" (NASB)

Where was this guy coming from? It looks like he was trying to say something profound, but really had no idea what Jesus was talking about. He may just have been excited about the future resurrection Jesus mentioned. Or maybe he was trying to say it's better to eat bread in the kingdom of God than enjoy a rich banquet now.

Perhaps he was spiritualizing what Jesus said to avoid inviting the poor to his house. Or he may have been expressing a common, but possibly unfounded, confidence that he would be part of that resurrection. Jesus may have known that, and he seized the opportunity to go deeper into their lives. Listen carefully to what people around you are saying, and take advantage of open doors to share the Word of God, even if you know it will make them uncomfortable.

God's problem with his invited guests

[16] *Jesus replied: "A certain man was preparing a great banquet and invited many guests.* [17] *At the time of the banquet he sent his servant to tell those who had been invited, 'Come, for everything is now ready.'*

Jesus was addressing a cherished Jewish belief. Most of the guests at that meal might not even realize what he was saying, but if they did, they probably left even angrier with Jesus. The Jews were the chosen people and were very proud of that. They resisted any possibility of Gentiles entering the kingdom. Now Jesus was saying that those chosen people—God's invited guests—will refuse his invitation. They may be chosen, but they still have free will. They are so wrapped up in things of the world that they are not interested in this banquet. They won't make it into the kingdom of heaven.

Then, as now, invitations were sent out in advance, with an RSVP expected. These guests had accepted the invitation, but when it came time to show up for the banquet, they all had excuses for not going.

¹⁸ *"But they all alike began to make excuses. The first said, 'I have just bought a field, and I must go and see it. Please excuse me.'* ¹⁹ *"Another said, 'I have just bought five yoke of oxen, and I'm on my way to try them out. Please excuse me.'* ²⁰ *"Still another said, 'I just got married, so I can't come.'*

The excuses haven't changed much in 2000 years:

- "I've just bought." Money and the things we buy with it often are more important to us than a relationship with the living God. If you have more money, you buy more, and you have more distractions.

- Houses and fields often take priority over God.

- Work—the five yoke of oxen—can become an all-consuming idol.

- Women, sex, and family are blessings from God. But Jesus still must be Lord. And when God calls, we have to answer his call.

They were courteous enough to ask to be excused, but it's not up to us to decide when we will respond to God. There is no excuse for refusing his invitation. Many today respond to an initial invitation to come to Jesus, but are full of excuses for not obeying him, and won't enter his kingdom. Beware of excessive confidence, such as the Jews had, that a response to an invitation years ago guarantees your place in the kingdom!

²¹ *"The servant came back and reported this to his master. Then the owner of the house became angry and*

ordered his servant, 'Go out quickly into the streets and alleys of the town and bring in the poor, the crippled, the blind and the lame.'

Did you notice something here? These are the same people Jesus said we should invite to our homes in verse 13! The Father is furious about the excuses made by those he invited to his banquet. Go out into the streets and alleys and invite everyone to Christ!

22 "'Sir,' the servant said, 'what you ordered has been done, but there is still room.'

23 "Then the master told his servant, 'Go out to the roads and country lanes and compel them to come in, so that my house will be full. 24 I tell you, not one of those who were invited will get a taste of my banquet.'"

God wants a full house! Are you inviting everyone to his house? To his banquet? Compel them to come in!

What an afternoon! All of this happened in the space of a few hours, in the home of someone who didn't even like Jesus, around a meal.

- Are you available to share the Word in homes, at meals, and in the daily life of your community? Or are you always stuck in church?

- Are you bound up in religious tradition? Or are you free to love and minister to those nobody else wants to deal with?

- Are you caught up in the typical climb up the corporate and social ladder? Or are you willing to humble yourself and let God lift you up?

- Are you available when God calls? What excuses do you usually make for disobedience?

11

You are the Salt of the Earth

Matthew 5:13

Jesus taught in the Beatitudes that part of life in the kingdom is being hungry, thirsty, meek, mournful, and poor in spirit—hardly someone you would expect to have a transforming impact on the world around them. And the blessed person is not well-received; in fact, they can expect to be persecuted. Our culture is very different from the world's. Indeed, in his prayer in John 17, Jesus says we are not *of* the world, but we are *sent into* the world, just as his Father sent him to this earth. In this dark and decaying world, he says we are the salt of the earth and the light of the world, reflecting kingdom values as righteous, merciful, and pure-hearted peacemakers.

The salt of the earth

[13] *"You are the salt of the earth. But if the salt loses its saltiness, how can it be made salty again? It is no longer*

good for anything, except to be thrown out and trampled underfoot.

When you accepted Jesus as Lord and Savior, you were given an all-inclusive package—these are not options you can select from:

- You were born again; your old life has passed away and everything is made new.
- Your sins were forgiven.
- You became a member of Jesus' body, the universal church.
- God sent you out as an ambassador of the King.
- God adopted you as his child.

Now Jesus adds two more: you *are* the salt of the earth, and, in the next verse, the light of the world. You aren't given the choice: "Would you like to be salt?" No, you *are* the salt of the earth—you, and every other believer.

The characteristics of salt

Salt is 40% sodium and 60% chloride, one of the most abundant minerals on Earth. It is mined from deposits left by ancient seas. It has even come to Earth in meteorites, but the most abundant source is the ocean. Salt has been used for thousands of years. Jesus doesn't expound on what it means to be salt, but we know that:

- Salt adds flavor; without salt, food is bland. A little salt goes a long way, enhancing the taste of other spices. It doesn't take much salt to season a whole meal. Paul encouraged us to have that impact in every interaction with others: *Let your conversation be always full of grace, seasoned with salt, so that you may know how to answer everyone* (Col. 4:6).

- Salt preserves and purifies. Jesus may have been thinking of Elisha's miracle in 2 Kings 2:21: *Then he went out to the spring and threw the salt into it, saying, "This is what the Lord says: 'I have healed this water. Never again will it cause death or make the land unproductive.'"*

- Salt cleanses and disinfects, whether in a wound or the house. In the past, salt would be rubbed on a newborn to cleanse it: *On the day you were born your cord was not cut, nor were you washed with water to make you clean, nor were you rubbed with salt or wrapped in cloths* (Ez. 16:4).

- Salt lowers the temperature at which water freezes. In cold climates, it makes streets and sidewalks safer by melting the snow and ice.

- In the right quantities, salt is beneficial to our health. In fact, you could say it is essential for good health.

Today, only 6% of salt is used in food. Some 68% is used in the chemical industry. There are around 14,000 commercial uses of salt. Internet pages give hundreds of common uses. Some of those are:

- Improving the flavor of coffee by removing the acid (put a little salt in the coffee basket)
- Removing rust (mixed with a little lemon juice)

- Removing stains from coffee or tea cups
- Relieving sore throats by gargling

Wonderful as salt is, to be of any use, it has to get out of the saltshaker. You can have a pantry full of salt, but it's worthless unless you take it out, fill the saltshaker, and put it on your food. There is more than enough "salt" (Christians) to season the whole world; the church possesses great potential to preserve and season. There is enough for your city as well.

But too much salt in one place is no good; it can choke out the life. If you consume too much, it can give you a heart attack. Jesus was familiar with the Dead Sea. It is lifeless because there is too much salt. Salt has to be spread out to be effective and life-giving. The problem is that most Christians don't leave the saltshaker (their church), and when they go into the world, they don't bring the savor of Jesus Christ.

Types of salt

- Table salt, which is mined from ancient dry seas.

- Sea salt, which comes from the ocean and is of better quality. It has more flavor and retains essential minerals and nutrients that are removed in refined table salt.

- Attention has recently focused on Himalayan salt, which is pink and only found in the mountains of Asia. It is ancient; some believe it dates to creation and the oceans that covered the earth before dry land was formed.

Jesus probably never heard of Himalayan salt. He most likely used a crude and impure form of sea salt, possibly from the Dead Sea. Which type of salt are you? Do you carry the savor of Jesus Christ? Or have you been so "refined" by the world that you have lost most of what makes salt valuable? Do you have deep roots in the rock of Jesus Christ, like Himalayan salt?

Salt in the Old Testament

There are three references to salt in the Old Testament law, which may help us understand what it meant to Jesus.

- *Season all your grain offerings with salt. Do not leave the salt of the covenant of your God out of your grain offerings; add salt to all your offerings* (Lev. 2:13).

- *Whatever is set aside from the holy offerings the Israelites present to the Lord I give to you and your sons and daughters as your perpetual share. It is an everlasting covenant of salt before the Lord for both you and your offspring"* (Num. 18:19).

- *When you have finished purifying it, you are to offer a young bull and a ram from the flock, both without defect. You are to offer them before the Lord, and the priests are to sprinkle salt on them and sacrifice them as a burnt offering to the Lord* (Ez. 43:23-24).

Even Jewish scholars are unsure of the meaning of a salt covenant and the exact purpose of salt being required in every offering, but we do know that:

- As opposed to leaven, which putrefies, salt preserves and was a sign of incorruption and purity.

- Like the covenant, salt is unchangeable and unalterable.

- In the Middle East, salt has been a symbol of friendship for millennia. If a man shared his salt with you, you could be sure he would do you no harm, leading to a common expression, "there is salt between us."

- The value of salt is evident in the saying "he is not worth his salt."

- In Eastern Orthodox churches, salt is a required ingredient in communion bread, reflecting this requirement of salt in an offering.

- In the traditional Roman Catholic rite of baptism, a few grains of salt are placed in the infant's mouth as a sign of wisdom. Salt is also added to holy water. As living sacrifices, we spiritually sprinkle ourselves with salt to purify ourselves and be acceptable to the Lord.

Jesus places a very high value on us when he says we are the salt of the earth. We become that essential ingredient when we offer ourselves as living sacrifices to God. We reflect God's unchangeable and unalterable covenant of forgiveness and reconciled relationship in our interactions with the world. We offer to "share the salt" in faithful relationships with those around us. Salt (and light) sacrifice themselves for the good of the larger community—it is impossible to get salt back once it has seasoned food, just as the energy spent to produce light cannot be reclaimed.

Tasteless salt

Given its value and importance, it's obvious why Jesus would have a very low opinion of salt that has lost its flavor. It is worthless! Jesus spoke about it various times.

"In the same way, those of you who do not give up everything you have cannot be my disciples. Salt is good, but if it loses its saltiness, how can it be made salty again? It is fit neither for the soil nor for the manure pile; it is thrown out. Whoever has ears to hear, let them hear." (Lk. 14:33–35)

Jesus is talking about our unique influence in the world. To be useful as salt (and then light), you have to retain your difference. Given that, scientifically, it is almost impossible for salt to lose its saltiness, what was Jesus thinking about? Salt loses its saltiness when it is contaminated or mixed with other minerals; it no longer acts to heal, preserve, or season. We are the salt. The disciple who is a friend of the world and doesn't renounce all his possessions (Lk. 14:33) loses his saltiness. The Christian who wants to walk the broad road gets contaminated and loses his effectiveness. The salt and the earth are two separate things, just as the Christian and the world are different. If we lose that difference, we lose our ability to impact the world. The salt mixes with the people of this earth to season and preserve them. The Earth needs salt. Without salt, it gets corrupted and deteriorates. Without salt, it is tasteless. Have you tasted food that is crying out for salt? In the same way, when our salt is functioning as it should, the earth cries out for it.

Following Jesus and being his representative in the world is costly. In comparison to our devotion to him, we should "hate" our families (Lk. 14:26–27). We need to be clear on what we are getting into before committing to being the salt of the earth. If we don't take into account the cost of discipleship and don't embrace kingdom culture, evidenced by inappropriate relationships with family and possessions, we become as useless as tasteless salt.

Jesus' warning is stern: *It is good neither for the soil nor for the manure pile. It is thrown away.* The Christian who loses his saltiness can't get it back. He is worthless. He started following Christ without counting the cost. He brings disgrace to the name of Jesus. He is like the person in the parable of the sower who receives the word with joy. At first, everything looks great (Lk. 8:1–15), but the cares of this life and the deceitfulness of riches rob him of his saltiness. This reminds me of the sobering words of Hebrews 6:4–6:

It is impossible for those who have once been enlightened, who have tasted the heavenly gift, who have shared in the Holy Spirit, who have tasted the goodness of the word of God and the powers of the coming age and who have fallen away, to be brought back to repentance. To their loss they are crucifying the Son of God all over again and subjecting him to public disgrace.

One more reference about the possibility of losing our saltiness

This is in the context of sin that could cause us or others to stumble:

"If anyone causes one of these little ones—those who believe in me—to stumble, it would be better for them if a large millstone were hung around their neck and they were thrown into the sea. If your hand causes you to stumble, cut it off. It is better for you to enter life maimed than with two hands to go into hell, where the fire never goes out. And if your foot causes you to stumble, cut it off. It is better for you to enter life crippled than to have two feet and be thrown into hell. And if your eye causes you to stumble, pluck it out. It is better for you to enter the kingdom of God with one eye than to have two eyes and be thrown into hell, where

"'the worms that eat them do not die,
   and the fire is not quenched.'

Everyone will be salted with fire. Salt is good, but if it loses its saltiness, how can you make it salty again? Have salt among yourselves, and be at peace with each other" (Mk. 9:42–50).

The first part of the last verse is almost identical to Luke 14, but in Mark, the teaching that precedes it is on the importance of avoiding sin, to the extreme of cutting off the hand or putting out the eye that causes you to sin. Jesus is saying that for things to get that bad, we have lost our saltiness. To avoid that, we must:

- Have salt in us—the Spirit's presence and a purified life. (Here we are not the salt, but we have the salt *in* us.) Without salt to give it flavor and preserve it from corruption, the church (or society) can easily fall into that grievous sin.

- Be at peace with each other. Something about the salt helps us live in peace, and that peace fosters holy living. When there are divisions and conflicts among us, we are more apt to fall into sin.

The "salt" that God uses in us is fire, to purify us and ensure we don't end up in the fires of hell. It could be the baptism of fire, the baptism of the Holy Spirit. We are to have salt between us, resulting in peaceful, positive relationships. This is the relational aspect of salt we noted in Middle Eastern society. We must be scrupulous in avoiding anything that would contaminate our salt and make us useless. If we lose our saltiness and cause a "little one" to stumble, we will be thrown out and trampled underfoot in the fire of hell. There is no way to return and be made salty again.

The Christian who fails to deal with sin in his life and lacks positive relationships with others has lost his salt, his ability to have a Christ-like impact on the world. God doesn't save us to be entertained in church. He saves us to impact the world around us. You are the salt of the earth. How many "tasteless" Christians do you know?

They may warm a chair in church and pay their tithes, but they are useless in God's kingdom. Are you worth your salt? God is patient and merciful, but don't test him or play games with him. *Whoever has ears to hear, let them hear.*

.

12

You are the Light of the World

Matthew 7:14–15

Another purpose of Jesus' disciple, parallel to the salt, is to be the light of the world.

An important biblical theme

John's Gospel (1:5–9) starts with the coming of the light to this dark world:

The light shines in the darkness, and the darkness has not overcome it. There was a man sent from God whose name was John. He came as a witness to testify concerning that light, so that through him all might believe. He himself was not the light; he came only as a witness to the light. The true light that gives light to everyone was coming into the world.

Jesus brought light to this world, in Judea, for a brief time:

"I am the light of the world. Whoever follows me will never walk in darkness, but will have the light of life" (Jn. 8:12).

While I am in the world, I am the light of the world." (Jn. 9:5)

Jesus gave his light to his disciples. When he returned to the Father, he left us to be the light of the world. Now there are millions of believers shining Jesus' light throughout the earth. We are light, and the darkness cannot overcome us. God's purpose was that we would bring light to everyone, as the Sermon on the Mount (Matthew 5) states:

[14] "You are the light of the world. A town built on a hill cannot be hidden.

We have seen that we are salt, which preserves life and gives it flavor. A little salt can season a large pot, just as one candle can light up a whole room. The world is a dark place. Despite attempts to light it up, it remains very dark spiritually. Don't expect the government or someone in the world to be light; that is the church's responsibility. We are the only true light in this world. The church should be that city set on a hill, known and visible to everyone. When we set out to build a church, we should make sure that it cannot be hidden.

Don't hide your light

[15] Neither do people light a lamp and put it under a bowl. Instead they put it on its stand, and it gives light to everyone in the house.

It doesn't make sense to turn on a lamp and then hide it under a box or bowl. It is positioned to give maximum light, especially if the room is very dark. One candle or small lamp can light up an entire room. We should position ourselves to provide the most light possible. We must be careful not to become an ingrown community that keeps the light to itself.

The light is good. It is cruel to leave people lost in darkness when we have the light they need. We should look for opportunities to shine our light; indeed, we *must* shine it!

For this is what the Lord has commanded us:

"'I have made you a light for the Gentiles,
    that you may bring salvation to the ends of the earth.'" (Acts 13:47)

How to shine your light

16 In the same way, let your light shine before others, that they may see your good deeds and glorify your Father in heaven.

Jesus commands us to shine our light before everyone. It is our responsibility to make sure we are shining brightly. Be proud of it. How can we best shine? With good deeds! More than programs and worship services in church, it is our good works that impact our community. We want the world to see them, but not to draw attention to us! The result should be that God is glorified. The world should see the Father in us. If we receive the glory, there is something wrong.

A lamp without oil (or unplugged) is worthless. When a bulb burns out, there is no more light. You can have a beautiful lamp, but without electricity, it is just a pretty ornament. There are Christians who look very spiritual, but their lamps are empty. They are walking in darkness. They are no different than the world around them.

Unfortunately, many Christians are not shining their light and are lacking in good deeds. They are robbing their Father of much glory!

How is your light?

- Do you shine in this world?

- How are your good deeds? And your church's deeds?

- When was the last time you heard an unbeliever praising God because of the church's good deeds?

- How can you change your life and your church to encourage more good deeds?

The eye: The lamp of the body

Later, in the same sermon, Jesus returns to this theme of light. We *are* the light, but there are some things we must do to keep that light burning:

"The eye is the lamp of the body. If your eyes are healthy, your whole body will be full of light. But if your eyes are unhealthy, your whole body will be full of darkness. If then the light within you is darkness, how great is that darkness!" (Matt. 6:22–23)

To shine in this dark world, we must keep an inner light burning. We have control over the light that enters our lives. It all depends on the eyes, what we are looking at, and having clear vision. One version says *"when your vision is clear"* and *"when your vision is foggy."* Too many people have foggy vision. They lack direction in their lives, walking around like blind men.

If you have worn glasses, you know what it's like: the first thing you reach for in the morning is your glasses. Without them, you can barely find the bathroom, and could easily trip and fall. The Bible is like those glasses; it sharpens our vision and helps us see things as God sees them. I have heard stories of people in undeveloped countries who have never heard of glasses—they have lived with foggy vision for years, but are unaware of any alternative. One day, someone comes to their village with glasses, and suddenly their vision is clear. It's like a whole new world!

I wore contacts or glasses for many years, and finally decided to have laser surgery. What a miracle! It was like new eyes! The Christian's goal is to have laser surgery on the heart, where the Word of God becomes such an integral part of our lives that, along with the Holy Spirit, we consistently walk with clear vision.

What is tragic is to have foggy vision and deny that there is a problem, claiming that everything is fine: *And if the light you think you have is darkness, how deep that darkness is!* (Matt. 6:23, NLT) The Christian who is deceived and has allowed darkness into his life experiences a darkness that is even worse than the world. He loses his effectiveness as light in the world and walks in darkness.

Luke 11:33–36 combines the two portions from Matthew:

"No one lights a lamp and puts it in a place where it will be hidden, or under a bowl. Instead they put it on its stand, so that those who come in may see the light. Your eye is the lamp of your body. When your eyes are healthy, your whole body also is full of light. But when they are unhealthy, your body also is full of darkness. See to it, then, that the light within you is not darkness. Therefore, if your whole body is full of light, and no part of it dark, it will be just as full of light as when a lamp shines its light on you."

"Your eye is a lamp that provides light for your body. When your eye is good, your whole body is filled with light. But when it is bad, your body is filled with darkness. Make sure that the light you think you have is not actually darkness. If you are filled with light, with no dark corners, then your whole life will be radiant, as though a floodlight were filling you with light." (NLT)

Jesus likes the metaphor of light! In Matthew, he stressed the importance of our influence on society; here, he focuses on the light's impact on our inner life.

Just as the light we shine in the world should cast out all darkness and bring light to everyone, so also the light within us should cast out all darkness and fill us with light. How does the light come into us? Through our eyes.

That light (or darkness) is the source of your words, thoughts, and actions.

How are your eyes? Do you fill your whole body with the darkness of computer, phone, and TV screens? Today, more than ever, we fill ourselves with filth and things that offend God. We lose our influence in the world as light, and make it impossible to walk in the light. If you have stumbled, it may mean you have an eye problem; you lack that inner light to illumine your path. Even though the sun is shining, you are walking in darkness.

Jesus answered, "Are there not twelve hours of daylight? Anyone who walks in the daytime will not stumble, for they see by this world's light. It is when a person walks at night that they stumble, for they have no light." (Jn. 11:9–10)

Have you stumbled? Jesus has a promise for you: If you walk in the daytime, in his light, you will not stumble.

Darkness or light?

This is the message we have heard from him and declare to you: God is light; in him there is no darkness at all. If we claim to have fellowship with him and yet walk in the darkness, we lie and do not live out the truth. But if we walk in the light, as he is in the light, we have fellowship with one another, and the blood of Jesus, his Son, purifies us from all sin (1 Jn. 1:5–7).

Unfortunately, many Christians want God's blessings, but at the same time fill their eyes with the perversity of darkness. John knew that many were Christians in name only; they say they know God, but walk in darkness. That person is deceived and is a liar, just like the father of lies. God is pure light; darkness cannot co-exist with him.

Two very important things happen to the person who walks in the light, which the hypocrite who walks in darkness can never experience:

1. Fellowship with other believers who are also walking in the light. If you lack that fellowship, it could be that you are walking in darkness, or perhaps the other person is lying, and he is the one walking in darkness.

2. Forgiveness of sins. Yes, we receive salvation and forgiveness by faith, but we also know that repentance is necessary. There is no forgiveness for the person who continues to practice sin and habitually walks in darkness. The person who is forgiven and walking in the light experiences purity and freedom.

How to remain in the light

Yet I am writing you a new command; its truth is seen in him and in you, because the darkness is passing and the true light is already shining.

Anyone who claims to be in the light but hates a brother or sister is still in the darkness. Anyone who loves their brother and sister lives in the light, and there is nothing in them to make them stumble. But anyone who hates a brother or sister is in the darkness and walks around in the darkness. They do not know where they are going, because the darkness has blinded them (1 Jn. 2:8–11).

If you say you are in the light, but lack love for your brother, you are deceived; you are still in darkness.

- The darkness is passing away; the light shining from the church should increasingly light up this dark world.

- Light fosters love and good relationships, and does not allow for hatred.

- The one who loves stays in the light.

- There is nothing in the person who loves and walks in the light that will cause them to stumble.

- Something is seriously wrong if a "Christian" hates his brother:

  o He is actually in the darkness

  o He is walking in darkness

  o He doesn't know where he is going

  o He has been blinded by darkness; an interesting concept. Instead of pure eyes that are open to the light, the one who walks in darkness ends up blind.

Sinful man resists the light

You might expect people to be drawn to the light, as insects are drawn to a light at night, but it's not that way:

This is the verdict: Light has come into the world, but people loved darkness instead of light because their deeds were evil. Everyone who does evil hates the light, and will not come into the light for fear that their deeds will be exposed. But whoever lives by the truth comes into the light, so that it may be seen plainly that what they have done has been done in the sight of God (Jn. 3:19–21).

We can expect the same response. How someone reacts to the light reveals whether they are living by the truth or doing evil. Jesus said the world would hate us (Jn. 17:14). Don't be surprised if people avoid you when you shine your light; they don't want their deeds to be exposed. But better to have the light reveal them now, because someday everyone's works will be exposed.

The light exposes everything (Mark 4:21–25)

21 He said to them, "Do you bring in a lamp to put it under a bowl or a bed? Instead, don't you put it on its stand? 22 For whatever is hidden is meant to be disclosed, and whatever is concealed is meant to be brought out into the open. 23 If anyone has ears to hear, let them hear."

Our lives and good deeds should expose corruption and hypocrisy in the government, the business world, and the church. Is there anything hidden in your life? In your family? In your church? Someday it will all be exposed. Better to deal with it now. Whether in your marriage or on your job, it is always better to be open about sin and take care of the situation. Cover-ups almost always end up making things much worse. It is a principle for all of life: *every secret will be brought to light* (NLT). Our lives should be transparent, with nothing to hide. Do you have secrets you don't want anyone to know about? What will happen when they are brought to light?

But their evil intentions will be exposed when the light shines on them (Eph. 5:13).

At first, the following two verses seem unrelated to the theme of light, but it says that Jesus *continued* with these words, or *added* them.

The measure you use

²⁴ *"Consider carefully what you hear," he continued. "With the measure you use, it will be measured to you—and even more.*

How do you treat others? Are you merciful with their failures? If you are harsh with them and their secrets and sins, God will be even harsher with you, as we saw with the parable of the unmerciful servant in Matthew 18:21–35. How do you respond when you find out about a secret your spouse has kept? Do you show them the same mercy you hope they will show you? How do you respond to your kids' secrets?

"Consider carefully what you hear" is another universal principle. Be careful about listening to lies and gossip. Some people are always trying to find out others' secrets. Listen to the truth. Be especially careful about what you hear—and believe—on the Internet.

²⁵ *Whoever has will be given more; whoever does not have, even what they have will be taken from them."*

Jesus says the same thing in Matthew 25:29, in the parable of the talents. The one who was given more talents and multiplied them was given more. The one who hid his talent and did nothing with it, out of fear of his master, lost what he had. The life that shines brightly will receive more light. The one who doesn't allow his light to shine will lose what little light he has. The person with a significant impact on his world, who brings much praise to his Lord with his good deeds, will be given more opportunities to do good deeds. If there is a lot of salt in your life and you have a big impact on your world, God will give you more opportunities to be salt. He will multiply the effect of that salt and light.

In context, what Jesus says here applies to our understanding of his word and his purposes. God will give even more understanding to the one who studies the Word and receives revelation from God, but the one who neglects to study and fails to seek understanding will lose the little he had.

Share what you receive from the Lord (Luke 8:16–18)

[16] *"No one lights a lamp and hides it in a clay jar or puts it under a bed. Instead, they put it on a stand, so that those who come in can see the light.* [17] *For there is nothing hidden that will not be disclosed, and nothing concealed that will not be known or brought out into the open.* [18] *Therefore consider carefully how you listen. Whoever has will be given more; whoever does not have, even what they think they have will be taken from them."*

This passage is very similar to Mark, but the emphasis here is on the need to proclaim the truth of God's Word. Jesus had just explained the parable of the sower and the seed (which is the Word). The light of the Gospel should enlighten everyone who hears our words. If you use every opportunity to share that truth, you will be given more opportunities. If you don't, you will lose the little ministry you had.

The same principle appears for a third time in Luke 19:26, in the parable of the minas. This is kingdom economics. It is the opposite of socialism, which takes from those who have much and gives to those who have little. We must carefully listen to the teaching and preaching of God's Word, to learn, understand, and then share it. God's gifts are not meant to be held onto, but to share: *But the seed on good soil stands for those with a noble and good heart, who hear the word, retain it, and by persevering produce a crop* (Lk. 8:15). It is God's will that you produce a hundredfold crop.

Walk in the light

Then Jesus told them, "You are going to have the light just a little while longer. Walk while you have the light, before darkness overtakes you. Whoever walks in the dark does not know where they are going. Believe in the light while you have the light, so that you may become children of light." When he had finished speaking, Jesus left and hid himself from them. I have come into the world as a light, so that no one who believes in me should stay in darkness (Jn. 12:35–36; 46).

If you have Jesus' light and are walking with him, you should have direction in your life and know where you are going. If you feel lost, it could be that you are walking in darkness and don't have fellowship with the light. If you don't walk daily in the light, the darkness can sneak up on you and surprise you.

And so we come back to the theme of these books: walking as Jesus walked. If we are going to be salt and light, we have to walk. We have to go into dark places, maintain our light and our distinctiveness, and be Jesus' presence in this world. We can make it very complicated, analyzing every little thing to see if it pleases God or not, or we can simply follow Jesus. His light will cast out all the darkness from your life. If you follow hard after Jesus, you will walk in his light and shine that light to the world.

13

Relationships in the Kingdom

Matthew 5:21–26, 38–42; 7:1–6, 12

Are you a murderer?

²¹ *"You have heard that it was said to the people long ago, 'You shall not murder, and anyone who murders will be subject to judgment.'*

Everyone knows that murder is forbidden in the Ten Commandments. "But I've never murdered anyone! I must be okay!" Maybe not, because Jesus holds his disciples to a much higher standard:

²² *But I tell you that anyone who is angry with a brother or sister will be subject to judgment. Again, anyone who says to a brother or sister, 'Raca,' is answerable to the court. And anyone who says, 'You fool!' will be in danger of the fire of hell.*

That doesn't seem all that serious; indeed, we might do this and not think anything about it:

- Get angry with a brother or sister.
- Insult someone (speak to them with contempt, call them names)
- Curse someone (call them a fool, or an idiot)

But this is a salvation issue! In reality, you are saying "I wish you were dead," and Jesus says you can be:

- Subject to judgment.
- Answerable to the court.
- In danger of the fire of hell.

There is murderous intent in your heart, and your words can effectively kill someone. Jesus takes the way we think about others and talk to them very seriously. Years later, the apostle John affirmed what the Master said: *Anyone who hates a brother or sister is a murderer, and you know that no murderer has eternal life residing in him* (1 Jn. 3:15).

Be reconciled before giving your offering

Healthy relationships are so important that Jesus commands us to get right with others before taking part in church services and offerings:

23 "Therefore, if you are offering your gift at the altar and there remember that your brother or sister has something against you, 24 leave your gift there in front of the altar. First go and be reconciled to them; then come and offer your gift.

You may not be in the wrong. You may be faithfully serving the Lord, but a brother has something against you. It is *your* responsibility to seek him out, talk to him, and restore the relationship. Right relationship is more important to Jesus than your offering. Can you imagine how much offerings would drop if people took Jesus seriously? Why do we ignore his commands?

Don't go to court!

²⁵ *"Settle matters quickly with your adversary who is taking you to court. Do it while you are still together on the way, or your adversary may hand you over to the judge, and the judge may hand you over to the officer, and you may be thrown into prison. ²⁶ Truly I tell you, you will not get out until you have paid the last penny.*

Here, it is not a brother, but an adversary, presumably someone outside the church. Jesus doesn't condemn the believer; he knows what the world is like. But he says there is no need to defend yourself, prove your innocence, and seek justice. Jesus' advice is:

- Resolve the issue as quickly as possible, even if you feel it is not entirely fair.

- Avoid the courts. Jesus doesn't trust the world's justice system. Good counsel for Christians who are quick to sue and take others to court!

And Jesus was no fan of prisons—apparently, he felt it was common to receive unjust and too lengthy sentences.

Eye for eye

A little later in the Sermon, Jesus returns to this theme of justice and retribution:

38 "You have heard that it was said, 'Eye for eye, and tooth for tooth.'"

Here Jesus quotes the Law, which was short on compassion and mercy:

But if there is serious injury, you are to take life for life, eye for eye, tooth for tooth, hand for hand, foot for foot, burn for burn, wound for wound, bruise for bruise (Ex. 21:23–25).

Anyone who injures their neighbor is to be injured in the same manner: fracture for fracture, eye for eye, tooth for tooth. The one who has inflicted the injury must suffer the same injury (Lev. 24:19–20).

Show no pity: life for life, eye for eye, tooth for tooth, hand for hand, foot for foot (Deut. 19:21).

That is strict justice, but Jesus introduces a radical new ethic, which is still radical today:

39 But I tell you, do not resist an evil person. If anyone slaps you on the right cheek, turn to them the other cheek also. 40 And if anyone wants to sue you and take your shirt, hand over your coat as well. 41 If anyone forces you to go one mile, go with them two miles. 42 Give to the one who asks you, and do not turn away from the one who wants to borrow from you.

Turn the other cheek

What a weakling! That person surely will be taken advantage of! Radical faith is required to trust that God will protect you and provide for you:

- Don't resist the evil person who wrongs you.

- Don't just allow him to slap you, turn the other cheek so he can slap that one also!

- If someone takes you to court for a small amount (a shirt), don't fight them—give them more than they're asking for (your coat as well)!

- If someone forces you to do something, voluntarily do twice as much as they ask!

- Always give or loan to the person who asks you for something.

We don't demand justice or retribution for what we have suffered. To walk like this, you need a radical faith that God will take care of you and provide for you. How far do you take that? Have you known anyone who took Jesus at his word? What would happen if Christians started living like this?

The Golden Rule

So in everything, do to others what you would have them do to you, for this sums up the Law and the Prophets (Matt. 7:12).

Jesus said in Matthew 22:37–40 that the Law and the Prophets (the teaching of the Old Testament) hinge on the commands to love God and love your neighbor as yourself. Treating others as you want them to treat you will help you to be "perfect," like your heavenly Father. Try it out to see how it can transform your relationships.

Radical love!

Jesus' teaching is very simple, but very difficult. We must deny ourselves, crucify our selfishness, and learn to love with the agape love that God has for us. That is almost impossible without the Holy Spirit and his fruit of love and patience, but it is an essential part of kingdom culture and walking like Jesus walked.

Love your enemy

It should be evident by now that Jesus has some extreme expectations for the way we relate to other people—a lifestyle which he clearly demonstrated. As in so much of his teaching, it goes completely against how the world— and most Christians—live. Now he commands us to do something that seems almost impossible:

43 "You have heard that it was said, 'Love your neighbor and hate your enemy.'

The Jews twisted God's Word, as many Christians do today. They quoted one part of this verse from the Law and ignored the part they found inconvenient:

"'Do not seek revenge or bear a grudge against anyone among your people, but love your neighbor as yourself. I am the Lord (Lev. 19:18).

The Old Testament never said to hate your enemy! In fact, the part of not seeking revenge or bearing a grudge sounds more like Jesus than the Law! Neither did the Old Testament command us to love our enemy, but Jesus exposes the limitations and hypocrisy of loving only your neighbor, and explains how God's love includes love for our enemies:

⁴⁴ But I tell you, love your enemies and pray for those who persecute you, ⁴⁵ that you may be children of your Father in heaven. He causes his sun to rise on the evil and the good, and sends rain on the righteous and the unrighteous. ⁴⁶ If you love those who love you, what reward will you get? Are not even the tax collectors doing that? ⁴⁷ And if you greet only your own people, what are you doing more than others? Do not even pagans do that? ⁴⁸ Be perfect, therefore, as your heavenly Father is perfect.

- Part of loving our enemies and those who persecute us is praying for them.

- God loves the vilest sinner with unconditional (agape) love.

- His love is displayed in what is called "common grace," things in this life which are God's gifts to all humanity. Here, Jesus mentions sunshine and rain.

- Of course, it is important to love our families and other believers, but even the worst sinners love those who love them. The real test of love is love for our enemies.

- This would be interesting to try in daily life: Don't greet only friends and other Christians, greet people who are very different from you as well!

Our love is shown in words, deeds, and prayers. Jesus knows he is setting a very high standard, but we have a very high calling: to be perfect! Yes, that is what he said. There is no excuse for mistreating others or for lacking love. Jesus calls us to be perfect, just as our heavenly Father is perfect. That requires great strength, self-control, and love.

14

Take Out the Speck!

Matthew 7:1–5

[1] "Do not judge, or you too will be judged. [2] For in the same way you judge others, you will be judged, and with the measure you use, it will be measured to you.

Do not judge anyone

These verses are often used to condemn any evaluation or correction of another person, but that is not what Jesus said—he just teaches that you must deal with your own sin before you try to help someone else. What standard do you use to measure others? Jesus has called us to be perfect. It is easy to hold others to that standard; it is harder to apply it to ourselves. Should we ever reach that perfection, it would be easy to become proud, but an important part of being perfect is humility.

- Do you measure your spouse and children (or your pastor, church, or employees) more harshly than yourself?

- Are you quick to judge others? Or do you show Jesus' love, patience, and tolerance in the face of their shortcomings?

- Do you know what it's like to be judged harshly (and unfairly) by someone?

Are there specks in your eyes?

I love how Jesus taught. Sometimes he would say something exaggerated or impossible just to get our attention and make his point:

³ "Why do you look at the speck of sawdust in your brother's eye and pay no attention to the plank in your own eye?

It could be a friend or your spouse, but there is an issue in their life. Nothing big, a speck. Nobody else sees it, and it doesn't bother the person, but it bothers you.

At the same time, you have a plank (or log) in your eye—something big, which everyone sees.

Jesus isn't saying that it is wrong to be concerned about your friend's problem. You're not acting in love if you see a speck in their eye and don't take it out. But first, there is something you need to do:

⁴ How can you say to your brother, 'Let me take the speck out of your eye,' when all the time there is a plank in your own eye? ⁵ You hypocrite, first take the plank out of your own eye, and then you will see clearly to remove the speck from your brother's eye.

It's fine to help someone who has a problem, like a speck in their eye. In fact, love demands that we help him. The problem is the tendency to see others' faults and ignore our own, which are often much worse. First, examine yourself and get your life in order. When you have taken the plank out of your eye (not to say that you are perfect, but you are working on it), then you can help someone else. You can seriously hurt the other person if you try to do it with a plank in your eye, and no one is going to receive your correction when it is apparent that you have a bigger problem. Jesus calls that person a hypocrite, like the Pharisees and others who were self-righteous and lacking humility and love.

Some questions for reflection

- Are you over-involved with others' problems?
  - Are you really helping them? Or are you hurting them?
  - Are you alienating them?

- Any planks in your eyes? What are they?
  - Can't think of any? Ask your spouse or a good friend if they see any. Assure them you won't hold it against them; they can be honest.
  - Then talk to the Lord about what they shared and ask him to help you get them out.
  - Humble yourself and ask your church or family for help. They may be biased, but take what they say seriously.

- Keeping a journal (or diary) can be risky, but if you are confident you can keep it private, write down the logs in your life, and how and when they are eliminated.
    o It can be helpful to think about how and when they have been dealt with in the past.
    o What do you learn about the nature of planks, and how God usually deals with them?

- With the plank gone, now you can see clearly to help others.
    o In love and humility, use what you learned by taking out your own plank.
    o In God's presence, reflect on your family and friends, and their specks. Give those specks over to the Lord and ask for discernment; is there something he wants you to do to help get them out?

This can be a humbling and painful process. Don't let the devil condemn you! You may have been walking around with these logs for years! Thank God that now you are aware of them! Thank him for wanting to get rid of them! And thank him that now you will be more useful, able to see clearly to help others.

Use discernment

[6] "Do not give dogs what is sacred; do not throw your pearls to pigs. If you do, they may trample them under their feet, and turn and tear you to pieces.

Discernment is not the same as judging. To obey this command, we need to evaluate people and decide who are dogs and pigs (no offense intended to dog lovers or pork fans). We are no fools. To love someone and not judge them does not mean that we give something sacred to a person who does not deserve it. If we do, they could turn around and tear us up! Someone who is ignorant and can't see the value of something could trample all over the precious gifts you offer them.

God is so good! He doesn't want you walking around with specks (or logs) in your eyes. He will help you get rid of them and give you the great privilege of working with him to help others get rid of theirs. Then we can see clearly and not stumble.

15

Who Will Cast the First Stone?

John 8:2–12

The book of Proverbs is full of warnings about adultery, like this one in 6:32:

A man who commits adultery has no sense; whoever does so destroys himself.

Under Old Testament law, adultery was one of several sins incurring the death penalty:

If a man is found sleeping with another man's wife, both the man who slept with her and the woman must die. You must purge the evil from Israel (Deut. 22:22).

Leviticus 20 lists various sexual practices outside of marriage that carry the death penalty. Jesus obeyed the law, and we know that stoning was still practiced in the first century—Stephen, in Acts 7, for example—but we never see Jesus stone anyone. Stoning someone was not so simple, either; Deuteronomy 17:1-7 lays out a fairly complicated process.

Killing an adulterer seems extreme to us, but God is serious about keeping his people pure and holy. John 8 offers an alternative response to blatant sin. Walking with Jesus requires much love and mercy, even for someone who violates one of the Ten Commandments, like an adulterer.

The ministry starts at dawn

² At dawn he appeared again in the temple courts, where all the people gathered around him, and he sat down to teach them.

Several times, we observe Jesus rising early: to pray, to meet the disciples on the beach (Jn. 21), and here, to teach the people. Many people were already in the temple at that hour, and Jesus was the main attraction. We are accustomed to standing to teach or preach, but, like the rabbis of that time, Jesus sat. And, unlike many preachers today, we don't see him very animated or shouting; his style was very calm.

Where is the adulterous man?

³ The teachers of the law and the Pharisees brought in a woman caught in adultery. They made her stand before the group ⁴ and said to Jesus, "Teacher, this woman was caught in the act of adultery. ⁵ In the Law Moses commanded us to stone such women. Now what do you say?"

What happened here presents several problems:

- Why were they keeping watch on the private lives of the people? Or did the man's wife (or the woman's husband) find them and tell the Pharisees?

- It seems disrespectful to interrupt Jesus' teaching with this distraction.

- Love and mercy are totally lacking; the poor woman is humiliated in front of the crowd.

- They conveniently ignore the part of the law that says both must die, reflecting women's inferior position at that time, something that God never intended. Jesus broke the norm with his honorable treatment of women.

Sometimes it's better to say nothing

⁶ They were using this question as a trap, in order to have a basis for accusing him. But Jesus bent down and started to write on the ground with his finger.

We don't know what Jesus wrote, but there have been many suggestions, among them "hypocrite," or possibly some of the sins of those teachers and Pharisees.

Walking as Jesus walked, we learn that sometimes it is better to stay quiet. Jesus knew this was a trap—if he let her go, they could accuse him of breaking the law. But it would be very ugly to stone her there, and they could report Jesus to the Romans, who didn't allow the Jews to carry out their own executions (Jn. 18:31).

Who will cast the first stone?

⁷ When they kept on questioning him, he straightened up and said to them, "Let any one of you who is without sin be the first to throw a stone at her."

Jesus affirmed the law—no one could accuse him of breaking it, and he also offered them the chance to leave with dignity. But, since they insisted on pressing the issue, Jesus was forced to point out their hypocrisy.

Some people are too ready to cast stones. They look for any minor fault to condemn and judge the person. Jesus offers us a radical alternative: The only one with the right to talk about others' sin is the one who is free of sin himself. Are you more apt to condemn and judge, or show compassion and forgiveness?

⁸ Again he stooped down and wrote on the ground.

There was no need to say a lot. Jesus didn't condemn them or rebuke them for their sin. He let the Holy Spirit do the work. Jesus was the only one who was sin-free, but instead of throwing stones, he stooped and wrote on the ground.

⁹ At this, those who heard began to go away one at a time, the older ones first, until only Jesus was left, with the woman still standing there.

The older ones were more conscious of their sin and humble enough to leave and not argue with Jesus. Would you be among the first to go? Or is it hard for you to humble yourself and confess that you're not perfect?

Jesus didn't come to condemn

¹⁰ Jesus straightened up and asked her, "Woman, where are they? Has no one condemned you?"

¹¹ "No one, sir," she said.

"Then neither do I condemn you," Jesus declared. "Go now and leave your life of sin."

There is no excuse for sin, but neither is there an excuse for a critical spirit that condemns and humiliates others. Love and mercy are as important as holiness.

Jesus saved her life—now she needs to repent and stop sinning. Unfortunately, many people whom Jesus forgives and offers a fresh start go back to their sin, or condemn others for less serious sins. John 3:17–21 says:

For God did not send his Son into the world to condemn the world, but to save the world through him. Whoever believes in him is not condemned, but whoever does not believe stands condemned already because they have not believed in the name of God's one and only Son. This is the verdict: Light has come into the world, but people loved darkness instead of light because their deeds were evil. Everyone who does evil hates the light, and will not come into the light for fear that their deeds will be exposed. But whoever lives by the truth comes into the light, so that it may be seen plainly that what they have done has been done in the sight of God.

Is there some sin you need to forsake? Jesus will help you walk free of sin.

When you follow Jesus, you will walk in the light

¹² *When Jesus spoke again to the people, he said, "I am the light of the world. Whoever follows me will never walk in darkness, but will have the light of life."*

It may be that the crowd was watching this whole exchange, and Jesus offered them a straightforward way to avoid sin: Follow him. Jesus is the light of the world. If we walk with him, it is impossible to walk in darkness; his light shines on our path.

In him was life, and that life was the light of all mankind. The light shines in the darkness, and the darkness has not overcome it (Jn. 1:4–5).

Are you walking in darkness? Would you say you have the light of life? Is your light shining? If not, are you really following Jesus? If you are walking in darkness, you are probably throwing stones, or you feel that someone is throwing stones at you. Jesus loves you. He doesn't throw stones. He receives you and accepts you as you are. If you feel humiliated and condemned by Pharisees, Jesus tells you: "Go now and leave your life of sin." Don't throw stones. Jesus rescued you from stoning; now show the same compassion and mercy to other sinners.

16

Think Like Jesus Thought about Money

Matthew 6:1–4; 19–34

Give: Freely and secretly

¹"Watch out! Don't do your good deeds publicly, to be admired by others, for you will lose the reward from your Father in heaven.

Good deeds are not optional for Jesus' followers—the next verse says "when," not "if." The issue is how we go about doing them, which reveals our heart and affects our reward. What we give in offerings to the Lord, and what we share with the needy (money or goods), betrays our attitude toward material things. If we realize that we are just stewards of what God has given us, generosity should come naturally. God is a giver, and a generous heart pleases him, but if we give expecting to receive more back, or to impress others with our spirituality, God is not pleased. Thank God, others will

121

benefit despite our wrong motives, but we lose our reward.

² "So when you give to the needy, do not announce it with trumpets, as the hypocrites do in the synagogues and on the streets, to be honored by others. Truly I tell you, they have received their reward in full. ³ But when you give to the needy, do not let your left hand know what your right hand is doing, ⁴ so that your giving may be in secret. Then your Father, who sees what is done in secret, will reward you.

The image of announcing our good deeds with trumpets is bizarre. Still, the sad truth is that some give to get the tax benefit the US government offers for donations, gain God's favor, or be recognized by others for our generosity. Some insist on a monument, plaque, bulletin notice, or even a building named after them! They don't know God's heart, and Jesus calls them hypocrites.

- What has God entrusted to you to manage as his steward? Are you being faithful with those blessings?
- Would you say you have a generous heart?
- Do you do good deeds hoping to be recognized by men? Or do you do them in secret?
- Have you given an offering or done some good deed and felt like nobody acknowledged it?

God sees everything you do in secret—good and bad—and surely will reward you.

Where is your treasure?

19 "Do not store up for yourselves treasures on earth, where moths and vermin destroy, and where thieves break in and steal. 20 But store up for yourselves treasures in heaven, where moths and vermin do not destroy, and where thieves do not break in and steal. 21 For where your treasure is, there your heart will be also.

Jesus doesn't say it is sinful to be rich or have possessions. It is a matter of priorities and what you store up. We tend to accumulate a lot of "stuff," which becomes obvious when we move. And we never use much of it! We moved to Costa Rica with two pallets of our belongings, and we don't miss any of what we sold or gave away! Many Christians would strongly protest that verse 21 does not apply to them: They may have a lot stored up in banks, the markets, and their homes, but they feel they are good Christians. Jesus would say they are deceived.

It is common sense: When you have a beautiful house or a new car, you have to get insurance, alarms, and locks to protect them. You worry about someone breaking into your home or scratching your vehicle. If you have money in the stock market, you follow the Dow Jones average. It is very freeing to have few possessions.

Our priority should be storing up treasures in heaven. But how?

- Do good works.

- Give away your money and possessions instead of storing them.
- Invest in other people (in evangelism, discipleship, and using your spiritual gifts to build up the church).

In other words, give toward whatever has eternal value.

Paul had Jesus' heart as he counseled the wealthy:

Command those who are rich in this present world not to be arrogant nor to put their hope in wealth, which is so uncertain, but to put their hope in God, who richly provides us with everything for our enjoyment. Command them to do good, to be rich in good deeds, and to be generous and willing to share. In this way they will lay up treasure for themselves as a firm foundation for the coming age, so that they may take hold of the life that is truly life (1 Tim. 6:17–19).

It is not a sin to have an abundance! God richly provides us with everything for our enjoyment! But it is very easy for the wealthy to put their hope and trust in their money and be proud and arrogant. They have a firm foundation for their earthly lives; now they need a firm foundation for life after death. That is truly living, not living the good life now. Paul echoes what Jesus said on storing up heavenly treasure:

- Do good.
- Be rich in good deeds.
- Be generous.
- Be willing to share.

Paul (unlike Jesus) doesn't tell them to sell everything and give to the poor, but they have to make their wealth available to Jesus to use as he wishes.

Where is your treasure?

- Are you always thinking of what you want to buy next?
- Do you have a lot of things stored up that you never use?
- Have you ever lost things to theft, fire, or natural disaster? How did you respond?
- Can you honestly say you have been obedient to Jesus' command not to store things up on earth?
- Whether your earthly treasure is little or much, are you generous and willing to share it?

The problem with our eyes

[22] *"The eye is the lamp of the body. If your eyes are healthy, your whole body will be full of light.* [23] *But if your eyes are unhealthy, your whole body will be full of darkness. If then the light within you is darkness, how great is that darkness!*

These verses appear to be out of context in a teaching on possessions. Of course, there is a broader application for anything that we see with our eyes, but I believe Jesus is talking about our tendency to covet what we see. He says the eye affects the whole body, just as where our time, energy, and heart are invested will affect our entire life. As your eyes give you light, a godly desire to serve the Lord and others will bring light to your whole life. The person with poor vision walks in darkness, just as selfishness and wrong motives rob us of love and generosity.

John spoke of the lust of the eye:

Do not love the world or anything in the world. If anyone loves the world, love for the Father is not in them. For everything in the world—the lust of the flesh, the lust of the eyes, and the pride of life—comes not from the Father but from the world. The world and its desires pass away, but whoever does the will of God lives forever (1 Jn. 2:15–17).

Most Christians claim to love God, but their actions betray them. They love the things of the world, and Jesus says the Father's love cannot dwell in them. They end up worshipping the god of materialism.

We must be careful with what we allow our eyes to see: Advertisements, TV, and the internet can trip us up and capture our hearts. Too often, the things of this world seem more real than heavenly treasures.

How are your eyes? Is your vision clouded by the attraction of all the material things that surround you? Are your eyes fixed on Jesus?

Impossible to serve two masters

[24] *"No one can serve two masters. Either you will hate the one and love the other, or you will be devoted to the one and despise the other. You cannot serve both God and money.*

Many people think they can be good Christians and still serve money, but Jesus says it is impossible—they are deceived and essentially saying that God's Word is not true. Of course, hardly anyone would admit that money is their master. It is easy to rationalize and have good excuses: "We never had anything when I was growing up," "I'm generous with the money I make." But God always loses out when we try to serve both him and money.

The options are to hate one and love the other, or be devoted to one and despise the other. If you truly love God and are devoted to him, you will hate and despise money. Or the other way around. That is a strong word for someone attracted to money and the things of this world. Someone once said: "Men can work for two bosses, but no slave can be the property of two masters. The essence of slavery is total possession and full-time service." God gives us what we need to serve him and others.

Don't be a slave to money! How can you tell if you are? Look at your thoughts, where you spend your time and energy, and your willingness to give to others. Jesus challenged a wealthy young man who wanted to know how to inherit eternal life:

Jesus answered, "If you want to be perfect, go, sell your possessions and give to the poor, and you will have treasure in heaven. Then come, follow me."

When the young man heard this, he went away sad, because he had great wealth.

Then Jesus said to his disciples, "Truly I tell you, it is hard for someone who is rich to enter the kingdom of heaven. Again I tell you, it is easier for a camel to go through the eye of a needle than for someone who is rich to enter the kingdom of God."

When the disciples heard this, they were greatly astonished and asked, "Who then can be saved?"

Jesus looked at them and said, "With man this is impossible, but with God all things are possible."

Peter answered him, "We have left everything to follow you! What then will there be for us?"

Jesus said to them, "Truly I tell you, at the renewal of all things, when the Son of Man sits on his glorious throne, you who have followed me will also sit on twelve thrones, judging the twelve tribes of Israel. And everyone who has left houses or brothers or sisters or father or mother or wife or children or fields for my sake will receive a hundred times as much and will inherit eternal life. But many who are first will be last, and many who are last will be first (Matt. 19:21–30).

To gain heavenly treasures, this man had to sell everything and give to the poor, and then follow Jesus. That may not be necessary for every Christian, but it does reveal what is most important to us. This man left sad, because it was clear he was a slave to money. Jesus does not say that in and of itself wealth is bad, but it can be very deceiving, and make it difficult to serve him as Lord. It is usually easier for a man who is poor in worldly things to wholeheartedly serve the Lord.

Jesus promises a heavenly reward for the apostles who had left everything to follow him: a hundred fold return, plus eternal life! Those who seem to have nothing in this life will be first in the kingdom, and the rich and powerful will be last.

17

How to be Rich Toward God

Luke 12:15–21 starts with this request: *"Teacher, tell my brother to divide the inheritance with me."*

Then [Jesus] said to them, "Watch out! Be on your guard against all kinds of greed; life does not consist in an abundance of possessions."

And he told them this parable: "The ground of a certain rich man yielded an abundant harvest. He thought to himself, 'What shall I do? I have no place to store my crops.'

"Then he said, 'This is what I'll do. I will tear down my barns and build bigger ones, and there I will store my surplus grain. And I'll say to myself, "You have plenty of grain laid up for many years. Take life easy; eat, drink and be merry."'

"But God said to him, 'You fool! This very night your life will be demanded from you. Then who will get what you have prepared for yourself?'

"This is how it will be with whoever stores up things for themselves but is not rich toward God."

It is a common theme in Jesus' teaching about money and material things: Don't store up things for yourself. Be on your guard against all kinds of greed. As opposed to what the world typically teaches us—and Christians often show in their actions, this life is not about an abundance of possessions. Jesus seems to say we need to be vigilant against various kinds of greed; there are a variety of ways that greed can creep up on us. Wealth is deceitful. Advertisements try to convince us that if we buy their product, life will be better, but it is a vicious cycle that never ends. It is never enough; there is always something else that we "need."

The man in the parable is not condemned for being rich; it could well be God's blessing which gave him a great harvest. The problem is his response to that abundance. It is easy to trust in what we have stored up (investments, insurance, savings, pensions) to give us a good life. The sad truth is that no one knows when this life will end. You cannot take it with you. Nor do we know when a fire, hurricane, or economic collapse could wipe out everything we have stored up.

What is Jesus' solution? Be rich towards God, and don't store up money and goods for yourself.

Do not worry

That parable served as an introduction to a teaching about worry. Jesus gave almost the same teaching in the Sermon on the Mount (Matthew 7):

[25] *"Therefore I tell you, do not worry about your life, what you will eat or drink; or about your body, what you will wear. Is not life more than food, and the body more than clothes?* [26] *Look at the birds of the air; they do not sow or reap or store away in barns, and yet your heavenly Father feeds them. Are you not much more valuable than they?* [27] *Can any one of you by worrying add a single hour to your life?*

[28] *"And why do you worry about clothes? See how the flowers of the field grow. They do not labor or spin.* [29] *Yet I tell you that not even Solomon in all his splendor was dressed like one of these.* [30] *If that is how God clothes the grass of the field, which is here today and tomorrow is thrown into the fire, will he not much more clothe you— you of little faith?* [31] *So do not worry, saying, 'What shall we eat?' or 'What shall we drink?' or 'What shall we wear?'* [32] *For the pagans run after all these things, and your heavenly Father knows that you need them.*

People who don't know God (and, unfortunately, many Christians) anxiously devote time and energy to getting many things. They run after them: buying and preparing food, dining out, dressing in the latest fashions. By God's grace, most of you reading this have no concerns about drinking water, where the next meal is coming from, or having enough clothes. We have full refrigerators and closets. We are free from those worries—but we still run after those things which *dominate the thoughts of unbelievers* (NTV)! Of course, we should give thanks for God's blessings. We don't have to feel guilty about enjoying what he has given us. God is not honored by us walking around in rags. But we must evaluate our attitude toward "things" in the light of this word, and be careful about what we buy. If you are in tough times right now, God wants to free you from worry; he promises to provide your needs.

I have to confess that it is hard to believe this promise when I see children dying of hunger in Africa. I would never say it is because they lack faith. I believe that as Christians, we are obligated to do everything possible to combat hunger in our communities and around the world. There is enough food on this earth to feed everyone; it is man's selfishness and sin that keep many from eating well. For example, if the US were to spend its defense budget on feeding the hungry, hunger would be eliminated.

Jesus says that worry betrays a lack of faith; in fact, worry is incompatible with faith. We didn't make ourselves, and we don't keep ourselves alive. God created us and now sustains us.

It is common sense: worry accomplishes nothing except to stress us out, and betrays a problem in our relationship with our Father, as this poem points out:

> Said the robin to the sparrow,
> "I would really like to know
> Why those anxious human beings
> rush around and worry so."
>
> Said the sparrow to the robin,
> "Friend, I think that it must be
> That they have no Heavenly Father
> such as cares for you and me."

I'm not sure if birds know God as their Father, but the message is clear: If we know him, how can we worry about these simple things of life? Yet even birds have to find their food; God provides, but we have to do our part, and plant crops, tend them, and harvest them.

The love of money

But godliness with contentment is great gain. For we brought nothing into the world, and we can take nothing out of it. But if we have food and clothing, we will be content with that. Those who want to get rich fall into temptation and a trap and into many foolish and harmful desires that plunge people into ruin and destruction. For the love of money is a root of all kinds of evil. Some people, eager for money, have wandered from the faith and pierced themselves with many griefs (1 Tim. 6:6–10).

That gain is not material!

- We are to be satisfied and content with what God has given us, and not covet more.
- Seeking riches opens the door to many temptations; it is easy to be trapped as slaves to acquiring more.
- Foolish and harmful desires plunge people into ruin and destruction.
- The love of money (not money itself) is the root of many kinds of evil.
- Greed leads many to wander from the faith and pierce themselves with griefs.

Perhaps you or someone you know has experienced the truth of this teaching.

Seek first the kingdom of God

33 But seek first his kingdom and his righteousness, and all these things will be given to you as well. 34 Therefore do not worry about tomorrow, for tomorrow will worry about itself. Each day has enough trouble of its own.

Once again, Jesus doesn't say that material things are bad. In fact, he promises to give us all the things he has just mentioned. We just need to let God decide what is necessary; there are many things we want, but don't need. There is nothing wrong with wanting the best for your family, but first we must seek God's kingdom and righteousness.

What is the most important thing that will be added to us? Many think about riches and material things, but in Luke, after that same saying, Jesus explains what it is:

"Do not be afraid, little flock, for your Father has been pleased to give you the kingdom. Sell your possessions and give to the poor. Provide purses for yourselves that will not wear out, a treasure in heaven that will never fail, where no thief comes near and no moth destroys. For where your treasure is, there your heart will be also" (Lk. 12:32–34).

Jesus says it is the kingdom of God that will be added to us! Preparing for that kingdom involves storing up unfailing treasures in heaven. How? By selling our possessions and giving to the poor. That command was not just for the rich young man! Where are the hearts of most Christians?

Jesus continues with a warning not to delay storing up heavenly treasures:

"Be dressed ready for service and keep your lamps burning, like servants waiting for their master to return from a wedding banquet, so that when he comes and knocks they can immediately open the door for him. It will be good for those servants whose master finds them watching when he comes. Truly I tell you, he will dress himself to serve, will have them recline at the table and will come and wait on them. It will be good for those servants whose master finds them ready, even if he comes in the middle of the night or toward daybreak. But understand this: If the owner of the house had known at what hour the thief was coming, he would not have let his house be broken into. You also must be ready, because the Son of Man will come at an hour when you do not expect him" (Lk. 12:35–40).

If we are busy making money and distracted by all our "toys" and the things of this world, there is a real risk that our eyes will be focused on them and we won't be ready. God gives us money and goods to manage as stewards. We must seek his will in how we use them and be faithful in blessing others with them. Jesus continues this teaching with the same theme of his return and the need to be prepared. Here, he has charged the manager with feeding his servants. God expects that those who have been blessed with abundance will be faithful and prudent in managing it to bless his people:

The Lord answered, "Who then is the faithful and wise manager, whom the master puts in charge of his servants to give them their food allowance at the proper time? It will be good for that servant whom the master finds doing so when he returns. Truly I tell you, he will put him in charge of all his possessions. But suppose the servant says to himself, 'My master is taking a long time in coming,' and he then begins to beat the other servants, both men and women, and to eat and drink and get drunk. The master of that servant will come on a day when he does not expect him and at an hour he is not aware of. He will cut him to pieces and assign him a place with the unbelievers (Lk. 12:42–46).

The believer who faithfully blesses those the Lord has entrusted to him will receive a position of great responsibility: God will put him in charge of all his possessions. The believer who selfishly abuses others, thinking only of himself and his pleasure, will be severely punished and sent to hell. Hell? Yes. This is a salvation issue.

Conclusion

This is a hard teaching for prosperity teachers who say God wants you rich. Neither Jesus nor any of the apostles were rich. Jesus' teaching goes totally against the materialism of this world—and of many Christians. There are some serious challenges here for wealthy Christians. We must remember Hebrews 13:5:

Keep your lives free from the love of money and be content with what you have, because God has said,

"Never will I leave you;
never will I forsake you."

18

Jesus and Money

Walking as Jesus walked involves our entire lives, not just the spiritual life. Here, Jesus teaches about our financial obligations to the less fortunate, the church, and the government. Jesus never had much money, and it wasn't important to him. Judas Iscariot was his treasurer. We don't know how he came to have that position, but he stole money (Jn. 12:6), and we, too, can be taken advantage of if we put our trust in the wrong person. Jesus understood that money is necessary for life in this world, but most of us give it too much importance.

New Testament teaching on money

The Old Testament treated wealth and material possessions as evidence of God's blessing. Many Christians adopt that perspective, but the New Testament has a rather negative attitude toward money and material things: They exist primarily to give and help those in need. It is hard to find a verse in the New Testament that says God wants you to be rich. We already saw several examples in the previous chapter, and these verses are representative:

- It is not necessarily sinful to be rich, but certain things are required of them: *Command those who are rich in this present world not to be arrogant nor to put their hope in wealth, which is so uncertain, but to put their hope in God, who richly provides us with everything for our enjoyment. Command them to do good, to be rich in good deeds, and to be generous and willing to share. In this way they will lay up treasure for themselves as a firm foundation for the coming age, so that they may take hold of the life that is truly life* (1 Tim. 6:17–19).

- James has stronger words: *Now listen, you rich people, weep and wail because of the misery that is coming on you. Your wealth has rotted, and moths have eaten your clothes. Your gold and silver are corroded. Their corrosion will testify against you and eat your flesh like fire. You have hoarded wealth in the last days. Look! The wages you failed to pay the workers who mowed your fields are crying out against you. The cries of the harvesters have reached the ears of the Lord Almighty. You have lived on earth in luxury and self-indulgence. You have fattened yourselves in the day of slaughter. You have condemned and murdered the innocent one, who was not opposing you* (Jas. 5:1–6).

- Revelation presents us with what seems like a contradiction:

- o For the church in Smyrna: *I know your
  afflictions and your poverty—yet you are
  rich! I know about the slander of those
  who say they are Jews and are not, but
  are a synagogue of Satan* (Rev. 2:9).

- o And the church in Laodicea: *You say, 'I
  am rich; I have acquired wealth and do
  not need a thing.' But you do not realize
  that you are wretched, pitiful, poor, blind
  and naked* (Rev. 3:17).

Our obligation to the less fortunate (Luke 16:19–31)

*[19] "There was a rich man who was dressed in purple and
fine linen and lived in luxury every day. [20] At his gate was
laid a beggar named Lazarus, covered with sores [21] and
longing to eat what fell from the rich man's table. Even
the dogs came and licked his sores.*

I can imagine this story preached in many contemporary
churches with a very different conclusion. Many
Christians would point to the rich man as blessed by God
and would identify with him. In that popular version, the
rich man shares the good news of salvation, prosperity,
and healing with Lazarus. The beggar gets saved, God
heals him, and blesses him with a good job in the rich
man's business. The sermon ends with Lazarus dressed
in the latest fashion and enjoying the good life, and the
assurance that God offers the same blessing to us.

But the parable Jesus told is radically different. The well-
dressed rich man had no time or compassion for the poor

beggar. It doesn't say, but he probably never gave him anything, even though he enjoyed a luxurious lifestyle every day. He never even offered Lazarus the crumbs from his table.

22 "The time came when the beggar died and the angels carried him to Abraham's side. The rich man also died and was buried. 23 In Hades, where he was in torment, he looked up and saw Abraham far away, with Lazarus by his side.

These are two extremes: one super-rich, the other indigent. The beggar is the hero of the story, and the rich man is the villain. We all die, which equalizes everyone. Lazarus was happy and pain-free, but the rich man arrived in hell naked, without his fine clothes or a penny of his wealth. Jesus never mentioned the religious practice of either the rich man or Lazarus. We can't assume that every rich person goes to hell or every poor person goes to heaven, but I think Jesus wanted to give the impression that it could be the case (in Mark 10:25, on another occasion, he said: *"It is easier for a camel to go through the eye of a needle than for someone who is rich to enter the kingdom of God."*).

What happened after death is radically different:

- Angels took Lazarus to Abraham's side, an exalted position.
- The rich man was buried (probably in a fancy tomb) and suffers torment in hell.

In his parable, Jesus allowed the rich man to see heaven, but that doesn't necessarily mean that is true in reality (although it would undoubtedly increase their torment).

24 So he called to him, 'Father Abraham, have pity on me and send Lazarus to dip the tip of his finger in water and cool my tongue, because I am in agony in this fire.'

25 "But Abraham replied, 'Son, remember that in your lifetime you received your good things, while Lazarus received bad things, but now he is comforted here and you are in agony. 26 And besides all this, between us and you a great chasm has been set in place, so that those who want to go from here to you cannot, nor can anyone cross over from there to us.'

It is very possible that the rich man rejected Lazarus' request for a crumb many times; now he asks Lazarus for relief from the fire (*the tip of his finger in water*). Before, he did not need mercy; now, he pleads for it.

Again, we can't deduce that if you receive good things in this life, you will go to hell, although Jesus did say: *"But woe to you who are rich, for you have already received your comfort. Woe to you who are well fed now, for you will go hungry. Woe to you who laugh now, for you will mourn and weep* (Lk. 6:24–25). Neither can we say that if you have it rough here, you will automatically go to heaven. But the minimum Jesus demands of the rich person is to have compassion and help the less fortunate. There is a strong tendency for rich people to trust in their riches and ignore the needs surrounding them. And there is comfort for the poor: God has great compassion for them and rewards them richly in heaven. If you are suffering now, God knows it, and there is hope for something much better in the future. Unfortunately, there is much injustice in the world, and many times the rich continue with the good life and ignore the needs of those around them. It may look like God does nothing, but God knows, and someday they will have to pay. Once you die, it is too late to ask for relief, mercy, or salvation from the torment of hell.

[27] "He answered, 'Then I beg you, father, send Lazarus to my family, [28] for I have five brothers. Let him warn them, so that they will not also come to this place of torment.'

[29] "Abraham replied, 'They have Moses and the Prophets; let them listen to them.'

[30] "'No, father Abraham,' he said, 'but if someone from the dead goes to them, they will repent.'

[31] "He said to him, 'If they do not listen to Moses and the Prophets, they will not be convinced even if someone rises from the dead.'"

The last verses of the passage don't have much to do with the theme of money, but speak of how hard it is for people who are comfortable in this world to believe the good news and help the needy. They had the Old Testament, but ignored it, and even Jesus' resurrection wasn't enough to change them.

Our obligation to God's work (Mark 12:41–44)

Unlike most churches today, no offering was collected in the temple; there were boxes where people could deposit their offering at their convenience. Nobody knew how much others gave, and that is how it should be in the church. One day, Jesus was watching the people. It seems he was seated by himself, and then called his disciples over:

41 Jesus sat down opposite the place where the offerings were put and watched the crowd putting their money into the temple treasury. Many rich people threw in large amounts. 42 But a poor widow came and put in two very small copper coins, worth only a few cents.

Once again, as in the previous example, Jesus puts down the rich and makes the poor widow the heroine.

43 Calling his disciples to him, Jesus said, "Truly I tell you, this poor widow has put more into the treasury than all the others. 44 They all gave out of their wealth; but she, out of her poverty, put in everything—all she had to live on."

God has a very different concept of what is important. He looks at the heart and the motive, and not the quantity. The widow gave everything; most of us give out of our abundance. Could it be that those who carefully give their 10%, thinking they have done well and God is pleased, are mistaken? So, does that mean that we must give everything we have? I don't think so, but it is important to be generous, and entrust everything we have to Jesus, be guided by him in how we use it, and truly live by faith.

Our obligation to the government: Matthew 22:15–22

Although the great Roman Empire oppressed his people, Jesus spoke very little about politics or our responsibilities to the government. Here he spoke only because the Pharisees pressured him:

15 Then the Pharisees went out and laid plans to trap him in his words. 16 They sent their disciples to him along with the Herodians. "Teacher," they said, "we know that you are a man of integrity and that you teach the way of God in accordance with the truth. You aren't swayed by others, because you pay no attention to who they are. 17 Tell us then, what is your opinion? Is it right to pay the imperial tax to Caesar or not?"

The Pharisees were opposed to the Romans; the Herodians were a political party that supported Herod Antipas. The two groups were always enemies, but here they united against Jesus (Luke says they sent spies). Despite their evil intentions, they spoke very highly about Jesus. They say that Jesus was a man:

- Of integrity
- Who taught the way of God in accordance with the truth
- Who wasn't swayed by others
- Who didn't focus on appearances

That is all true, but were they serious, or just flattering him? Be careful of flattery; God can help you detect and avoid that trap. They know that if Jesus says you don't have to pay taxes, they could accuse him of rebellion before the authorities. But he could lose his popular support and be seen as a traitor to his country and religion if he seems to sympathize with the Romans. Many resented the fact that their taxes helped maintain pagan temples and the luxurious lifestyle of the upper classes of Rome.

18 But Jesus, knowing their evil intent, said, "You hypocrites, why are you trying to trap me? 19 Show me the coin used for paying the tax." They brought him a denarius, 20 and he asked them, "Whose image is this? And whose inscription?"

21 "Caesar's," they replied.

Then he said to them, "So give back to Caesar what is Caesar's, and to God what is God's."

Jesus forces them to respond to their question with an obvious answer, and in the process, confirms our responsibility to pay taxes. It perfectly silenced his enemies, and he escaped their trap. It gives us a general principle: we must be faithful in paying our taxes and not break the law to avoid them. In the same way, we must give God what belongs to him. The two are separate, and it is important to maintain that distinction. The truth is that we are citizens of both an earthly and a heavenly kingdom.

Jesus never intended this to be a comprehensive teaching on giving, and the passage raises several questions:

- All money has the government's imprint. Does that mean we should give them all of it? Obviously not!

- No money has God's image ("In God we trust" doesn't count!). Does that mean we give no money to God? Of course not!

- How do we figure out what belongs to God? Who decides whether we have fulfilled our obligation? *We* are the ones who bear God's image; we must offer our entire lives to God!

22 When they heard this, they were amazed. So they left him and went away.

Jesus is so amazing! Without arguing or condemning anyone, he always had exactly the right words to respond to any situation! May he help us do the same!

God can also provide the money we need to pay taxes and obey the law. There is an interesting story in Matthew 17:24–27:

24 After Jesus and his disciples arrived in Capernaum, the collectors of the two-drachma temple tax came to Peter and asked, "Doesn't your teacher pay the temple tax?"

25 "Yes, he does," he replied.

When Peter came into the house, Jesus was the first to speak. "What do you think, Simon?" he asked. "From whom do the kings of the earth collect duty and taxes—from their own children or from others?"

26 "From others," Peter answered.

"Then the children are exempt," Jesus said to him. [27] *"But so that we may not cause offense, go to the lake and throw out your line. Take the first fish you catch; open its mouth and you will find a four-drachma coin. Take it and give it to them for my tax and yours."*

In this case, it was the temple tax, something Jesus implies should not have been charged to believers. Characteristically, Jesus already knows what they said to Peter, and has an unusual provision: a coin in a fish's mouth. Paying taxes is important to God, although Jesus does not seem too enthusiastic about it, and we can trust that he will provide the money to pay them.

How are you doing in these three areas?

- Do you identify more with the rich man or Lazarus? Is there a Lazarus near you whom you can help?

- If there are wealthy people in your congregation, how should you treat them? Which of the two versions I gave of this parable is closest to what you are used to hearing in your church?

- Do you feel satisfied because you give generous offerings? Does it require faith to do so? Do you know what it is like to give everything, to give until it hurts? Not because someone on TV pressures you to, but because God puts it in your heart.

- Can you confidently say that you are giving God what belongs to him? Are you robbing "Caesar" because you're not paying the taxes you should be?

19

Walking with Jesus in a "Den of Thieves"

John 2:13-25

It's obvious that kingdom culture is radically different than the world's culture. We resist the pressure to pursue wealth and material possessions. The children of the King are meek peacemakers, who love and forgive others. But it's not always peaceful in the kingdom:

From the days of John the Baptist until now the kingdom of heaven suffers violence, and violent men take it by force (Matt. 11:12, NASB).

The kingdom is also a battlefield. Demonically inspired people try to take it by force. They can't, but it is a battle. Sometimes we have to rise up to defend our King and kingdom values. Someone, for example, had to resist Hitler. There is a place for anger and the courage to enter the battle in our culture. In this passage, we will see how

Jesus navigated a den of thieves, where the kingdom of light confronted the kingdom of darkness.

¹³ When it was almost time for the Jewish Passover, Jesus went up to Jerusalem.¹⁴ In the temple courts he found people selling cattle, sheep and doves, and others sitting at tables exchanging money. ¹⁵ So he made a whip out of cords, and drove all from the temple courts, both sheep and cattle; he scattered the coins of the money changers and overturned their tables. ¹⁶ To those who sold doves he said, "Get these out of here! Stop turning my Father's house into a market!" ¹⁷ His disciples remembered that it is written: "Zeal for your house will consume me."

Zeal for his Father's house

This was not the first time Jesus had witnessed this disgrace, but you often have to calm down, control your anger, and wait for the right time and way to express it. One of the most important lessons of this passage is that anger is not sin; there may even be times when it is appropriate to violently confront the forces of evil. This is not the meek and mild Jesus of the paintings! His disciples saw him consumed with zeal for his Father's house. He didn't care about the money changers' losses; he purposely threw their money all over the floor. Who knows what happened to those coins? It may have been a free-for-all that morning. We have already seen that money held little importance for Jesus.

Anger and zeal are part of the King's character and the culture of his kingdom, described in many Old Testament passages and Revelation. This is the angriest we see Jesus. Why?

He called the temple a "den of thieves." They charged too much for the convenience of buying the doves, sheep, and cattle required for the sacrifices in the temple. The money changers, who exchanged foreign money for local coins, took advantage of the foreigners with high commissions.

Jesus drove them *all* from the temple. God's house should not be a market; it is a house of prayer, and Jesus condemned anything that would make the temple a marketplace. Aside from the buying and selling, imagine the noise, the excrement, and the stench of all those animals.

Is it okay to sell things in churches today?

- What about bookstores in churches? Or cafes? Even Starbucks?
- What about food sales to raise funds for church programs?
- Should invited preachers or musicians be allowed to sell their books or other material?

Almost all the opinions I read on the Internet justify some sales within the church building. True, in Christ *we* are the temple; God doesn't dwell in buildings, and our buildings are not holy, as the temple in Jerusalem was holy. God gave detailed instructions for the construction of that temple. But isn't anything problematic that detracts from the function of that building as a house of prayer and worship? When it becomes a market, we take away from that holy purpose.

Two purifications of the temple?

I want to pause here to reflect on a question many have about the temple cleansing. John's gospel places it at the beginning of Jesus' ministry; all he says is that *it was almost time for the Jewish Passover.* But which Passover? It is hard to see the connection to the miracle in Cana in the previous passage, or with Nicodemus' visit in John 3. It may be that this was the *last* Passover Jesus celebrated, after the triumphal entry, where Matthew places it (21:12–13):

Jesus entered the temple courts and drove out all who were buying and selling there. He overturned the tables of the money changers and the benches of those selling doves. "It is written," he said to them, "'My house will be called a house of prayer,' but you are making it 'a den of robbers.'"

Luke and Mark also place it during that last week of his ministry; Mark says explicitly it was Monday, after the triumphal entry:

The next day as they were leaving Bethany, Jesus was hungry. Seeing in the distance a fig tree in leaf, he went to find out if it had any fruit. When he reached it, he found nothing but leaves, because it was not the season for figs. Then he said to the tree, "May no one ever eat fruit from you again." And his disciples heard him say it.

On reaching Jerusalem, Jesus entered the temple courts and began driving out those who were buying and selling there. He overturned the tables of the money changers and the benches of those selling doves, and would not allow anyone to carry merchandise through the temple courts. And as he taught them, he said, "Is it not written: 'My house will be called a house of prayer for all nations'? But you have made it 'a den of robbers.'" (Mk. 11:12–17)

When John's temple cleansing took place may not be that important to most people, but it is a good example of the need to interpret the Scriptures carefully. It seems unlikely that Jesus would cleanse the temple twice. At the beginning of his ministry, he was careful not to call too much attention to himself—why would he do something so provocative so early? It would make more sense at the end of his ministry, when he already had many enemies. Indeed, after this, they wanted to kill him:

The chief priests and the teachers of the law heard this and began looking for a way to kill him, for they feared him, because the whole crowd was amazed at his teaching (Mk. 11:18).

Mark had a broader perspective than Matthew (who wrote for the Jews), and quotes Jesus saying that the temple is a house of prayer *"for all nations."* Jesus was already including Gentiles among God's people! Luke has the shortest reference:

When Jesus entered the temple courts, he began to drive out those who were selling. "It is written," he said to them, "'My house will be a house of prayer'; but you have made it 'a den of robbers.'" (Lk. 19:45–46)

It doesn't change the message; it is not that critical where we place the cleansing in John, but I believe it is the same event that the synoptic gospels place during the last week of Jesus' life. Perhaps John wanted to present the prophecy of Jesus' resurrection at the beginning.

The Jews demand a sign

We return to John 2 and the uproar Jesus caused in the temple. It is interesting to imagine the reaction of the common people; I am sure some of them were happy that someone had confronted these abuses. Of course, the merchants and temple leaders (who probably took a cut from the money earned) were furious, but instead of arresting Jesus, they demanded a sign that would authorize him to do this:

18 The Jews then responded to him, "What sign can you show us to prove your authority to do all this?"

19 Jesus answered them, "Destroy this temple, and I will raise it again in three days."

20 They replied, "It has taken forty-six years to build this temple, and you are going to raise it in three days?"

The fact that the temple was his Father's house should have been enough! But Jesus loves to confuse his critics, and offers them a very impressive sign: he challenges them to destroy the temple, and he would raise it again in three days. To see this sign, first they had to destroy the temple, something they obviously were not going to do. But Jesus took advantage of the opportunity to talk about his resurrection:

²¹ *But the temple he had spoken of was his body.* ²² *After he was raised from the dead, his disciples recalled what he had said. Then they believed the scripture and the words that Jesus had spoken.*

²³ *Now while he was in Jerusalem at the Passover Festival, many people saw the signs he was performing and believed in his name.*

Jesus didn't provide what the leaders requested, who, unlike his disciples, probably never connected the promise of raising the temple with his resurrection. But Jesus did do many signs that week, and much to the leaders' dismay, many believed in him.

What does it mean that Jesus "knew what was in each person"?

²⁴ *But Jesus would not entrust himself to them, for he knew all people.* ²⁵ *He did not need any testimony about mankind, for he knew what was in each person.*

The people believed in Jesus, but he didn't believe in them. Why?

Interestingly, both verses (22 and 23) say that they believed in Jesus, but it seems that the disciples' faith (v. 22) was more reasoned and mature, based on the Old Testament Scriptures and Jesus' words, and confirmed by his resurrection. This was one more step in the process of establishing them in a firm faith. On the other hand, *"many people"* believed in him during the Passover because they *"saw the signs he was performing."* Faith based only on signs and miracles is notoriously weak. It could be that the same people who praised Jesus the day before at his triumphal entry shouted "crucify him" a few days later. Jesus *"would not entrust himself to them"* because he knew how changeable humans can be. He knew what was in their hearts, as he says in John 6:64 about his disciples: *"Yet there are some of you who do not believe."* Jesus had known from the beginning which of them did not believe and who would betray him. He seems to imply that several of the Twelve did not believe in him, and one of them was a profound disappointment and a traitor. The truth is that Jesus completely knows you, which can bring much comfort or make you very uncomfortable—he knows your sincerity and what is in your heart.

After verse 25, John goes directly to the story of Nicodemus: *Now there was a Pharisee, a man named Nicodemus who was a member of the Jewish ruling council* (Jn. 3:1). That may be why John placed the temple cleansing here: The controversies with the Pharisees and other leaders, and their lack of faith, contrasts with Nicodemus. Jesus could see his heart and knew he was sincere and had faith, although not a saving faith; he had to learn what it means to be born again.

We don't need to be negative, suspicious, and cynical of people. We know that we are all sinners with a mixture of motives in our hearts:

The heart is deceitful above all things and beyond cure. Who can understand it? (Jer. 17:9)

The answer is obvious: Jesus! He knows what we are like, which is why he said we need to be shrewd and careful:

I am sending you out like sheep among wolves. Therefore be as shrewd as snakes and as innocent as doves. Be on your guard; you will be handed over to the local councils and be flogged in the synagogues (Matt. 10:16–17).

Being innocent does not mean being foolish. Knowing what people are like, we still need to love them and trust God to protect us.

Jesus was grieved and angered by the way his own people profaned his Father's house. There he was, probably after three years of ministry, and his impact seemed minimal. No wonder he responded with such anger! No wonder he didn't trust the people! There was a limit to his patience—one day his anger will be poured out on this sinful world. Be careful of turning what should be a place of prayer and worship into a business or market. What would happen if Jesus showed up at church and emptied the cash registers, ripped out the credit card readers, and threw out everyone who was buying or selling? Are there dens of thieves in your town? How can you walk like Jesus walked in that situation?

20

Never Alone

John 14

Crowds always followed Jesus, and much of his teaching, like the Sermon on the Mount, was directed to them. On other occasions, like the dinner party in Luke 14, Jesus shared with smaller groups, which often included his critics, the Pharisees and teachers of the law. Here, he is with his disciples in the intimacy of the Upper Room. It is only hours before his betrayal and arrest, and Jesus wants to share his heart with them. In light of his imminent death and ascension, he assures them that in God's kingdom, you are never alone.

Let not your heart be troubled

¹ *"Do not let your hearts be troubled. You believe in God; believe also in me.*

There will be plenty of reasons to be troubled: the disciples' world will be destroyed as they watch their Master judged and crucified. Jesus would have even more reason to be troubled, but he had three simple words for them:

- *Do not let your hearts be troubled.* It is a command. This chapter is full of reasons not to be troubled. You may be facing a challenging situation; walking like Jesus doesn't exempt you from them. There are times when we have to walk with him to Calvary, but we must fight the anguish and pain, and not allow our hearts to be troubled. Anguish is born of fear. Fill your heart with God's Word, praises, and the Holy Spirit, and there will be no place for the anguish.

- *Believe (trust) in God.* Jesus could have peace as he went to the cross because he had faith that his Father would resurrect him. Hopefully, you have experienced God's faithfulness and have a firm faith. He will never leave you or forsake you. Don't put your trust in man; trust in God. Is it a command or a declaration? It could be both: They already had faith in the almighty God of the Jews, now they can confidently have that same faith in Jesus, since they are equal. Or it could simply be a command to have faith in God and his Son.

- *Believe (trust) in [Jesus].* He is your older brother, your high priest, who was tempted in every way as you are. He is interceding for you at God's right hand.

Your life may not be going as you had hoped. Your world is shattered, and your heart is broken. You don't understand what is happening. You may be troubled and in anguish, but Jesus loves you and is in control. He wants the best for you. He has a plan and purpose for your life. There are jewels for you in this chapter, but Jesus knows that to receive them, you must be free of that anguish and have a living faith.

Walk by faith and not by sight

² My Father's house has many rooms; if that were not so, would I have told you that I am going there to prepare a place for you? ³ And if I go and prepare a place for you, I will come back and take you to be with me that you also may be where I am.

We learn to walk like Jesus walked while we are on this earth, but his plan is that we would walk together for all eternity. He wants you with him, and right now he is preparing a special place for you. Many people dream of owning a home. That is a special blessing, but if you live in a cramped apartment, don't worry, you will have a better place than any earthly mansion.

Jesus wants to fill you with that hope and expectancy. Lies and deceit surround us in this world, but you can trust in Jesus' word; he always tells the truth. Do you have a solid faith in heaven? How does it make you feel to know that someday Jesus will come to take you with him to that place? There is no better place than being with Jesus; many of us enjoy his presence in the secret place of prayer and during worship services in church. It is a small taste of what we are going to experience for eternity. Don't you want your whole family with you in that place? Share this word with them so that they can have the same hope.

Jesus *is* the way

⁴ You know the way to the place where I am going."

If you read the first book in this series, you may remember one of the first steps in walking with Jesus: entering through the narrow gate and walking the narrow road (Matt. 7:13–14). These disciples spent three years walking that road with Jesus; they should know it well. If we keep going on that road, we pass through death and enter directly into Jesus' presence.

⁵ Thomas said to him, "Lord, we don't know where you are going, so how can we know the way?"

⁶ Jesus answered, "I am the way and the truth and the life. No one comes to the Father except through me. ⁷ If you really know me, you will know my Father as well. From now on, you do know him and have seen him."

When we think of a road, we think of something physical, like a street. Too many times, the Christian walk is presented as a formula: Pray, read the Bible, go to church, and avoid sin. Those are good things; they are things we do while we are on the way, but the way is a person, it is Jesus. He is everything: The way, the truth, and the life. It is fashionable to say there are many roads to heaven; the important thing is to have a sincere faith in what you believe, whether it is Muhammad or Buddha. But Jesus says that he is the *only* way to the Father.

Thomas had already spent three years on the road, and still didn't know the way. There are "Christians" today who are like Thomas, always looking for a new experience, a more anointed church, or a prophetic word; they don't realize that all they need is Jesus. Christ said: *"If you (plural) really know me;"* apparently he knew that, after three years of intimate fellowship, it was possible that they really didn't know him. It could be your situation as well: you have tried to do everything right, you have carefully read this book and put its teachings into practice, but you really don't know Jesus. You are not convinced that God and his Word are real, and you are not experiencing a supernatural life. You may have sought life in relationships, money, or the good life. Real life is only found in a relationship with Jesus.

8 Philip said, "Lord, show us the Father and that will be enough for us."

Is Philip deaf? Jesus just said that they have already known and seen the Father because they have seen him. But the human tendency is to always want something more: More blessings, more influence, more power, or a higher position. "Lord, give me a good job and that will be enough for me. Give me a new house and that will be enough." But if it is not Jesus that we are seeking, it will never be enough. There will always be something else that you want. Think about the simplicity of those years that Philip spent with Jesus! You don't need anything more than intimacy with Christ!

9 Jesus answered: "Don't you know me, Philip, even after I have been among you such a long time? Anyone who has seen me has seen the Father. How can you say, 'Show us the Father'? 10 Don't you believe that I am in the Father, and that the Father is in me? The words I say to you I do not speak on my own authority. Rather, it is the

Father, living in me, who is doing his work. [11] Believe me when I say that I am in the Father and the Father is in me; or at least believe on the evidence of the works themselves.

Later that same night, in his prayer in John 17, Jesus would say that in the same way the Father is in Jesus, Jesus is in us, and we are in the Father. That union is the basis of our success on this Christian walk.

There are several important things in these verses:

- Jesus speaks of word and deed. We repeatedly see that combination in his ministry. Many people are all talk; our words should build up and communicate God's heart, but words without deeds are just talk. We must demonstrate God's power in our good works.

- It's great when someone believes the Word, but some have to see to believe. Our works should give testimony of who God is.

- In verse 10, Jesus says: *The words I say to you I do not speak on my own authority.* Too many Christians (even pastors) speak on their own authority. We should follow Jesus' example and speak only the words God gives us when we speak in his name. If he doesn't give us a word, it is better to stay quiet.

- There is a common belief that it is not possible to see God (that is what Exodus 33:20 and 1

Timothy 6:15–17 say). It is part of Muslims' and others' arguments that Jesus cannot be divine. But here Jesus says that if you have seen him, you have seen the Father. Since God is spirit, it is not possible to see him physically, and we could not stand the weight of his glory. We do see the complete revelation of who God is, not in Jesus' flesh, but through his words, deeds, and spirit.

The same Father who did his works in Jesus can do his works in you as well, which brings us to the next point.

You will not only walk like Jesus walked, you will do the works he did

[12] *Very truly I tell you, whoever believes in me will do the works I have been doing, and they will do even greater things than these, because I am going to the Father.*

To add emphasis, Jesus says, "Very truly, I tell you. Almost every promise comes with a condition, but the only condition here is to believe in Jesus. He *wants* us to do his works. It should be our normal experience, not something unusual.

What were the works Jesus did? Healings, deliverances, resurrections, multiplication of food, and walking on water. I have heard that "greater" means "more." Obviously, with millions doing his works, there will be more, but the clear sense is that they would also be more impressive.

Don't you want your son to do more with his life than you did? God is not so jealous that he would say, "Nobody can do anything greater than what Jesus did in this world." No, the son (or the disciple) should do more than his teacher.

The promise is very clear, so why don't we see more of his works? It would seem that the problem is with our faith; we really don't believe in Jesus, and we don't expect him to do these works through us. The truth is that at times, in some places, we have seen Jesus' works, and greater. He doesn't require someone special, just a clean vessel available to act in faith. The next verse offers us another explanation for the lack of greater works.

The power of prayer

13 And I will do whatever you ask in my name, so that the Father may be glorified in the Son. 14 You may ask me for anything in my name, and I will do it.

Jesus repeats the promise to add emphasis, and adds the word *"anything"* to make the promise inclusive. Some people use this promise to justify asking for and claiming a big house and a new car—selfish, materialistic things. But the promise is given in the context of doing the works Jesus did. And there is a very important condition: to ask *"in my name."* That doesn't mean ending your request with the words "in Jesus' name" (although it's fine to end a prayer that way). To ask in his name means asking in accordance with Jesus' heart and will, as if Jesus himself were doing the work.

God is ready to answer our prayers because he wants to glorify his Son, which means that the request should bring glory to Jesus. If our motive in praying is to glorify ourselves, a church, or a ministry, God probably won't answer it. But if it brings great glory to Jesus, the heavens are opened to pour out God's power. Prayer is the means to release the power to do Jesus' works. It is so important that Jesus shares his own prayer in chapter 17, and repeats this same promise in John 16:

23 In that day you will no longer ask me anything. Very truly I tell you, my Father will give you whatever you ask in my name. 24 Until now you have not asked for anything in my name. Ask and you will receive, and your joy will be complete.

Once again, Jesus uses the words *"very truly I tell you"* to emphasize the certainty of the promise. Before, they didn't need to pray to Jesus, because he was there with them—through prayer, we have the same access to Jesus that the disciples enjoyed. Our joy is important to Jesus! He knows that it is a blessing to receive and to give. He delights in answering our prayers and seeing our joy.

How is your joy? Is it complete? How is your prayer life? Do you believe you are asking in accordance with Jesus' heart and will? Do you see many answers? Do you want to see Jesus glorified in answered prayer, or are you only thinking about what you can get?

The importance of obedience

Continuing in John 14:

19 Before long, the world will not see me anymore, but you will see me. Because I live, you also will live. 20 On that day you will realize that I am in my Father, and you are in me, and I am in you.

Look at what Jesus is saying!

The world won't see Jesus > The believer sees him

Christ lives > We live

Jesus is in the Father > We are in Christ, and he is in us

So, we get all the blessings! We see Jesus, we live, we are in him, and he is in us. When Jesus returns to the Father, the disciples will become aware of this intimate relationship with Christ, perhaps through the Holy Spirit dwelling in them. Jesus could be speaking of his post-resurrection appearances, or that they will see him spiritually.

Each one leads to an intimate relationship with Jesus, where we see him, share in his life, and are united to him. It should result in loving him. So how do you know for sure if you love him?

[21] *Whoever has my commands and keeps them is the one who loves me. The one who loves me will be loved by my Father, and I too will love them and show myself to them."*

We know that God already loved us so much that he sent Jesus to this world to save us, but this verse says that we experience more of God's love when we express our love in obedience. It is easy to say that we love Jesus and sing about it in church, but the test is in daily life, in temptation, and in making those hard decisions to obey his Word when we don't feel like it. We are not talking about forced obedience, out of fear, or just to avoid punishment. If we love Jesus, we have to make his commandments ours. We delight in them, like the Psalmist often wrote about God's law. To obey them, we have to know them. Do you study the Bible to learn about his commands? Do you put the Word into practice? Do you listen for the Spirit's voice and obey him?

How great to have all these blessings from God, but it is here that we examine ourselves to see if we are truly walking as Christ walked. How is your obedience? If you are not experiencing God's love, could there be a problem there?

22 Then Judas (not Judas Iscariot) said, "But, Lord, why do you intend to show yourself to us and not to the world?"

That is a different attitude! Most people are only concerned about what *they* can experience with the Lord. Judas is thinking about the mission he understood Jesus to have—it seems contradictory to him that Jesus would not show himself to the world. Characteristically, Jesus doesn't answer his question.

23 Jesus replied, "Anyone who loves me will obey my teaching. My Father will love them, and we will come to them and make our home with them. 24 Anyone who does not love me will not obey my teaching. These words you hear are not my own; they belong to the Father who sent me.

Jesus' answer seems to be: "I will show myself to those who love me and obey my word." He doesn't say it, but maybe now it is the disciples' responsibility to show Jesus to the world, through their words and the works that Jesus did.

If you love someone, you want to please them and do what is important to them. Obeying Jesus is not a burden, but something we want to do. We look for every opportunity to obey. Jesus adds even more weight to his words—they are from the one who has authority over him, from his Father. Disobedience not only dishonors Jesus but also his Father.

The peace of Christ

²⁷ Peace I leave with you; my peace I give you. I do not give to you as the world gives. Do not let your hearts be troubled and do not be afraid.

Peace can be given. Jesus has supernatural peace to leave with us. The world has peace, but it is temporary. We may feel peace in a quiet place, in nature, in our spouse's arms, with good music, or after success in some project. But that peace relies on the circumstances, and many things can steal that peace. Christ's peace is a deep peace that lasts despite the circumstances. His peace guards our hearts from anguish and gives us courage to confront life's problems. That perfect love and peace cast all the fear out of our hearts.

Here Jesus returns to what he said at the start, in verse one. We don't know exactly how Jesus shared this, but apparently, he is close to the end of this portion.

"I will not say much more to you, for the prince of this world is coming."

²⁸ "You heard me say, 'I am going away and I am coming back to you.' If you loved me, you would be glad that I am going to the Father, for the Father is greater than I. ²⁹ I have told you now before it happens, so that when it does happen you will believe. ³⁰ I will not say much more to you, for the prince of this world is coming. He has no hold over me, ³¹ but he comes so that the world may learn that I love the Father and do exactly what my Father has commanded me.

The hour of trial is close. Jesus may have already seen the anxiety on his disciples' faces. They don't like the idea of Jesus going away. Selfishly, we want Jesus to always be with us. Like the separation from a loved one, whether in a move or death, it hurts. But if we love that person, we are happy, knowing that the believer goes to God's presence when he dies, and that new job or marriage will result in many blessings for that person. So Jesus hopes that they can rejoice with him, knowing that he is going home, going back to his Father.

There is order in the divinity. The three persons are God, but Jesus clearly says here that the Father is greater than he is. Jesus submits to his authority, and the Holy Spirit acts according to the will of the Father and the Son. Jesus voluntarily submitted to the devil, even though the devil had no dominion over Jesus. Christ calls him the *"prince of this world"* because God has given him authority on this earth. To undermine that authority, Jesus will obey his Father and die as a sacrifice on the cross to bring in a new kingdom and take back what the devil stole.

Jesus has shared what will happen, hoping that they will remember when it does happen, and their faith will be strengthened. May we have Jesus' heart to do exactly what God commands us to do. It is a testimony to the world of our love for God, denying ourselves to please him.

"Come now; let us leave."

It is not easy to leave the beautiful fellowship of the Upper Room, the communion with beloved brothers, and Jesus' sweet presence. But sooner or later, we have to come down from the mountain and go onto the battlefield. Jesus knows what is waiting for him and has tried to prepare his disciples. Unfortunately, they will still be filled with discouragement, anguish, and unbelief in the coming days.

21

Walking Like Jesus is Not Easy

John 15 & 16

We have seen how kingdom culture is totally different than the world. It is not surprising, then, that the believer who faithfully puts these teachings into practice would be misunderstood and persecuted. We want big churches and the respect of people around us. Years ago, in traditionally Catholic countries, non-Catholics were used to persecution. In many cases, that has changed, so that in some cases it is popular to be an evangelical. In traditionally Christian countries, believers are often surprised at how many are opposed to biblical teaching. In Muslim countries, conversion to Christianity can result in death. We are quick to complain about "persecution," but Jesus clearly said that we will suffer in this world. That night in the Upper Room, Jesus tried to prepare his disciples for the opposition they would face.

The world hates us (John 15)

¹⁸ "If the world hates you, keep in mind that it hated me first.

Didn't crowds follow Jesus and celebrate him as king as he triumphantly entered Jerusalem on Palm Sunday? Sure, but some of that same crowd yelled "crucify him" later that week, and Jesus was left with only 120 after his resurrection. Of course, entire countries have been impacted by revivals, and leaders of various countries have been Jesus' disciples. But the world system is completely opposed to the values of the kingdom of God, and hates Christ and his followers.

¹⁹ If you belonged to the world, it would love you as its own. As it is, you do not belong to the world, but I have chosen you out of the world. That is why the world hates you.

It is so easy for us to forget that we are not of this world! Jesus took us out of the world! If you are seeking the world's approval, you will find it very hard to obey Jesus. Many Christians today want both: what the world offers and God's blessings. But that is impossible; they are entirely different cultures. The world talks about tolerance, but in reality, there is little tolerance in the world for people in the kingdom. The world loves its own, but hates us.

²⁰ Remember what I told you: 'A servant is not greater than his master.' If they persecuted me, they will persecute you also. If they obeyed my teaching, they will obey yours also. ²¹ They will treat you this way because of my name, for they do not know the one who sent me.

If they persecuted Jesus, they will persecute you, his disciple. Do you really think we can escape the persecution that Jesus endured? Like father, like son. Like master, so his servant. Like Jesus, so his disciple. It is not surprising that they reject you, because they do not know God. Don't take it personally—there is something about Jesus that the person in the kingdom of darkness hates. The person with an open heart to receive and obey Jesus' teachings will also receive and obey our teachings. The characteristic of Jesus' disciple, of kingdom culture, is obedience.

No excuse for their sin

²² If I had not come and spoken to them, they would not be guilty of sin; but now they have no excuse for their sin.²³ Whoever hates me hates my Father as well. ²⁴ If I had not done among them the works no one else did, they would not be guilty of sin. As it is, they have seen, and yet they have hated both me and my Father.

Jesus doesn't suggest that this is a theology of the destiny of those who have never heard the Gospel; he is simply giving some conditions in which someone would not be guilty of sin:

- If Jesus had not come.
- If he had never spoken to them.
- If he had not done the works that no one else had done.

A person is responsible for what they have seen and heard. The person who has never heard about God and his only Son may be judged by a different standard (see Romans 2:12–16). It is the person who has seen and heard the message—and rejected it—who is condemned. Indeed, they hate Jesus, and the one who hates Jesus also hates his Father.

Why would anyone hate Jesus, someone so full of love and wisdom, who only did good? Healing, saving, blessing, and setting people free? Because their hearts are hardened, they are blinded by the devil, and they love their sin and the things of the world. We are in a spiritual battle, and Satan is the deceiver and father of lies.

25 But this is to fulfill what is written in their Law: 'They hated me without reason.'

If it seems that someone hates you for no reason, don't be discouraged; that is just the way our fallen race is. There was no reason for the hatred toward Jesus, and there is no reason for the hatred many have for his disciples. Nevertheless, it is our responsibility to make sure there is no legitimate reason for the world's hatred (for example, hypocrisy). Peter wrote to Christians who were suffering (1 Pet. 4:12–19):

Dear friends, do not be surprised at the fiery ordeal that has come on you to test you, as though something strange were happening to you. But rejoice inasmuch as you participate in the sufferings of Christ, so that you may be overjoyed when his glory is revealed. If you are insulted because of the name of Christ, you are blessed, for the Spirit of glory and of God rests on you. If you suffer, it should not be as a murderer or thief or any other kind of criminal, or even as a meddler. However, if you suffer as a Christian, do not be ashamed, but praise God that you bear that name. For it is time for judgment to begin with God's household; and if it begins with us, what will the outcome be for those who do not obey the gospel of God? And,

"If it is hard for the righteous to be saved,
  what will become of the ungodly and the sinner?"

So then, those who suffer according to God's will should commit themselves to their faithful Creator and continue to do good.

So your faith does not fail (John 16)

¹ "All this I have told you so that you will not fall away.

It is better to know ahead of time what could happen to us. Facing all that hatred and persecution, our faith could fail. Jesus knows it is a very real possibility that even his disciples would fall away. Are there unexpected things happening in your life? Things that are tripping you up? Have you thought of giving up your faith? We are in the last days, and the persecution is only going to get worse, to the point that it will be almost impossible to endure it. Jesus said: *"If those days had not been cut short, no one would survive, but for the sake of the elect those days will be shortened"* (Matt. 24:22).

² They will put you out of the synagogue; in fact, the time is coming when anyone who kills you will think they are offering a service to God.³ They will do such things because they have not known the Father or me. ⁴ I have told you this, so that when their time comes you will remember that I warned you about them. I did not tell you this from the beginning because I was with you.

If you knew from the beginning how hard it would be to follow Jesus, would you still follow him? In the suffering, it is easy to forget that Jesus already warned us. These were religious people (in this case, zealous Jews), but today it might be someone who claims to be a Christian and believes that he is serving God—the devil's deception can be that extreme. We must be prepared: *"Then you will be handed over to be persecuted and put to death, and you will be hated by all nations because of me. At that time many will turn away from the faith and will betray and hate each other, and many false prophets will appear and deceive many people. Because of the increase of wickedness, the love of most will grow cold, but the one who stands firm to the end will be saved"* (Matt. 24:9–13).

There are many false prophets today. Are you under a pastor's covering, submitted to the spiritual authority God has placed over you? Someone with the discernment to identify them? How is your love? Don't let it grow cold.

Joy in the midst of suffering

¹⁹ Jesus saw that they wanted to ask him about this, so he said to them, "Are you asking one another what I meant when I said, 'In a little while you will see me no more, and then after a little while you will see me'? ²⁰ Very truly I tell you, you will weep and mourn while the world rejoices. You will grieve, but your grief will turn to joy.

It is common sense: they hated Jesus and will be happy to see him killed. There will be pain and sadness. Weeping may endure for the night, but joy comes in the morning. When you see Jesus, when he returns, your pain will be replaced by joy. There are things in this world that dismay us, but in Jesus, that sadness is changed to joy.

21 A woman giving birth to a child has pain because her time has come; but when her baby is born she forgets the anguish because of her joy that a child is born into the world.22 So with you: Now is your time of grief, but I will see you again and you will rejoice, and no one will take away your joy.

You may be "pregnant" now—there could be anguish as you struggle to grow in the Lord and give birth to a work of God. How great to know that someday we will be with the Lord forever. In his presence, there is joy that no one can take away.

32 "A time is coming and in fact has come when you will be scattered, each to your own home. You will leave me all alone. Yet I am not alone, for my Father is with me.

How quickly we forget our Savior and abandon him! This prophecy would be fulfilled within a few hours. It is hard to be faithful to Christ when he gets crucified and your own life is in danger. Jesus knows our weaknesses and our tendency to run from difficulties, but despite the unfaithfulness of these disciples—and, at times, ours—he remains faithful.

Christ has overcome the world

33 "I have told you these things, so that in me you may have peace. In this world you will have trouble. But take heart! I have overcome the world."

Kingdom culture is very different from that of the world, and, unfortunately, from what is taught in many churches. The Christian life is not pain-free; in fact, we will face hardships in this world. But Christ leaves us with these encouraging words:

- In him, we will find peace in the storm, especially as we reflect on his words and the Scriptures. Your peace does not come from circumstances or material things. This is a deeper peace, which comes from Jesus' presence in you.
- Are you facing trials? There is nothing wrong with you, and you are probably not in sin. The sad reality is that it is part of being in this world.
- Christ wants to encourage you. He is with you and knows what is happening. You are not alone.
- He has overcome the world, and shares that victory with you. In Christ, we are more than conquerors!

22

The Comforter

John 14–16

J esus is preparing his disciples for an important transition: from his physical presence, to the presence of the Holy Spirit. The book of Acts is full of teaching on the Spirit. In fact, it has often been called "The Acts of the Holy Spirit." We will study Acts in the fourth volume in this series. There is also rich teaching in the epistles, but this is what Jesus shared during his earthly life, primarily in the Upper Room. There is surprisingly little teaching on the Spirit recorded in the Gospels. For an in-depth study of the Holy Spirit, read my book What Ever Happened to the Baptism in the Holy Spirit?

The Comforter given to those who obey Jesus (John 14)

15 "If you love me, keep my commands. 16 And I will ask the Father, and he will give you another advocate to help you and be with you forever— 17 the Spirit of truth. The world cannot accept him, because it neither sees him nor knows him. But you know him, for he lives with you and will be in you. 18 I will not leave you as orphans; I will come to you.

Jesus spoke about us doing his works—and greater—and of his readiness to answer our prayers. Now he moves to another dimension of our relationship with him.

He does not say "you love me," but "*if* you love me." For Jesus, the only sure proof of our love is our obedience. We walk with Jesus and experience his love, with hearts full of love and gratitude for all he has done for us. That love motivates us to listen for his voice and study his written word, anxious to obey and put into practice everything he has said. The more you love Jesus and obey him, the more you will experience of the Spirit.

When Christ is sure of our love and obedience, he asks the Father for a special gift. Acts 5:32 confirms the important role our obedience plays in receiving that gift: *"We are witnesses of these things, and so is the Holy Spirit, whom God has given to those who obey him."* When Christ asks his Father for something, we can be confident he will answer. The Spirit is a gift that you may receive when you accept Jesus, or may be given after you have walked with Christ for a while. Sin, disobedience, and rebellion quench the Spirit. God intends that he would never leave us, that he would always be with us, but as King Saul found out (1 Sam. 16:14), the Spirit can depart from us.

There is an intimate connection between Christ and the Spirit. Here, Christ says he will not leave us as orphans, but will come to us, speaking of the coming of the Spirit. The Spirit is a person we can get to know, who lives with us and is in us. The Spirit is a mystery to the unbeliever because they cannot see him. Since they do not know

Christ, they cannot know the Spirit. For us, he is the Spirit of truth, who leads us into all truth.

Comforter and Teacher

25 "All this I have spoken while still with you. 26 But the Advocate, the Holy Spirit, whom the Father will send in my name, will teach you all things and will remind you of everything I have said to you.

The Spirit has various functions, among them the Comforter who is at our side—and inside us—to help us (*paraklete* in Greek). In verse 16, Jesus said he is *another* Comforter; Jesus is one comforter, and the Spirit has a similar ministry. He is also a Teacher, who teaches us far more than Christ could in his three years here, although Jesus' teachings have a special importance. The Spirit also reminds us of everything that Jesus said.

Have you experienced the healing ministry of the Comforter? How? Has he taught you anything lately? Do you seek time free from the cellphone and other distractions to listen to his voice?

Witnesses (John 15)

26 "When the Advocate comes, whom I will send to you from the Father—the Spirit of truth who goes out from the Father—he will testify about me. 27 And you also must testify, for you have been with me from the beginning.

One of the central ministries of the Spirit is to testify about Jesus. We can pray that the Spirit would work in an unbeliever's heart and testify to people, especially in countries where evangelism is not permitted. It sounds very spiritual to say that we will leave that work to the Holy Spirit, but Jesus says that we also are to give testimony—it does not say *"may* testify," but *"will* testify." We evangelize together with the Spirit.

The Spirit also helps us testify in court: *"But when they arrest you, do not worry about what to say or how to say it. At that time you will be given what to say, for it will not be you speaking, but the Spirit of your Father speaking through you"* (Matt. 10:19–20).

Did you experience the Spirit's testimony before you accepted Christ? Have you seen the work of the Spirit in unbelievers' lives? How are you doing with your witness for Christ? When you witness, you will feel more of the Spirit's presence. One of the greatest blessings of being a Christian is to see the Spirit work in an unbeliever's life.

Better that Christ would go away (John 16)

⁵Now I am going to him who sent me. None of you asks me, 'Where are you going?' ⁶ Rather, you are filled with grief because I have said these things. ⁷ But very truly I tell you, it is for your good that I am going away. Unless I go away, the Advocate will not come to you; but if I go, I will send him to you.

In John 14:6, Thomas asks the way to where Jesus is going. The disciples did not always seem too bright, and were more interested in what would happen in their own lives than what was going to happen with Jesus. Instead of rejoicing that Jesus would return to the glory of heaven (14:28), they were sad.

How beautiful it would be to still have Christ here on earth, to talk with him and take part in his ministry! But Jesus says that we have something even better: The Spirit, who dwells in us and is always with us, Counselor, Comforter, Teacher, and source of spiritual power 24/7. While Christ was still here on earth, he could not send the Spirit in his fullness.

The Spirit convicts the world

⁸ When he comes, he will prove the world to be in the wrong about sin and righteousness and judgment:⁹ about sin, because people do not believe in me; ¹⁰ about righteousness, because I am going to the Father, where you can see me no longer;¹¹ and about judgment, because the prince of this world now stands condemned.

The Bible never says it is our job to convict others of their sin and need of a Savior. That is the Spirit's work, on three levels:

1. Regarding sin, because they do not believe in Jesus. Yes, that is a sin.

2. Regarding righteousness, because Jesus went to the Father, and we can no longer see him.

3. Regarding judgment, because Satan has already been judged.

¹² "I have much more to say to you, more than you can now bear. ¹³ But when he, the Spirit of truth, comes, he will guide you into all the truth. He will not speak on his own; he will speak only what he hears, and he will tell you what is yet to come. ¹⁴ He will glorify me because it is from me that he will receive what he will make known to you. ¹⁵ All that belongs to the Father is mine. That is why I said the Spirit will receive from me what he will make known to you."

Like Jesus, the Spirit does not speak on his own authority, but instead guides us to all truth. He will share many things with us that Christ did not have the opportunity to share.

There are times when God knows we are not ready to receive something, and waits until we are ready. In the same way, we should have that sensitivity to know if something is too much for another person. Sometimes we talk too much. Once again, Jesus says the Spirit will guide us into all truth, and adds another dimension to that revelation: he will announce the things to come.

We also have two other facets of his ministry:

- He takes what belongs to Jesus and makes it known to us. There is an exchange among the three persons of the Trinity (in saying that, Jesus affirms its reality): Everything that the Father has is Christ's; the Spirit freely takes it and gives it to us.
- In that process, the Spirit glorifies Jesus. His desire is always to glorify the Father and the Son.

Rivers of living water (John 7)

³⁷ On the last and greatest day of the festival, Jesus stood and said in a loud voice, "Let anyone who is thirsty come to me and drink. ³⁸ Whoever believes in me, as Scripture has said, rivers of living water will flow from within them." *39* By this he meant the Spirit, whom those who believed in him were later to receive. Up to that time the Spirit had not been given, since Jesus had not yet been glorified.

"*Later.*" That may be the reason Jesus did not talk much about the Spirit during his ministry; he would only be given after Jesus was glorified.

Who receives the Spirit? "*Whoever believes in me.*" *Those who believed in him.* Do you believe in Jesus? Then the gift of the Spirit is for you! How interesting that the disciples did all those miracles without the Spirit's presence in their lives; it was only in the power of Jesus' name.

Jesus describes the Spirit as rivers of living water flowing from inside us. Have you felt those rivers? Many are happy with a few drops or a shower once in a while. Some may get immersed in those waters during an anointed church service. But Jesus spoke of rivers; something powerful flowing out from inside you that would bring life, refreshment, and God's presence to your family, work, and community. Let's pray for a flood of those living waters!

Breathe on me (John 20)

21 Again Jesus said, "Peace be with you! As the Father has sent me, I am sending you." 22 And with that he breathed on them and said, "Receive the Holy Spirit. 23 If you forgive anyone's sins, their sins are forgiven; if you do not forgive them, they are not forgiven."

Now Jesus has risen from the dead and can give the Spirit to his disciples.

Three important things accompany the Spirit's breath:

- Jesus' peace fills us.
- It is not just to enjoy his presence, but to enter the world with God's power. In the same way the Father sent Jesus into the world, Jesus sends us into the world.
- Acting in his name, we have the authority to forgive sins—or not forgive them. This has caused confusion, because we know that only God can forgive sin. The simple answer is that Christ sends us into the world with the power of the Spirit to proclaim the forgiveness of sins through faith in Jesus' sacrifice on the cross. We can assure those who accept that salvation that they are forgiven; we never want to give the impression that someone is forgiven unless they have accepted Christ. Those who reject the message of salvation are not forgiven.

Christ breathed on them to receive the Spirit, but they were not baptized in the Spirit until Pentecost. In fact, in the following passage (Acts 1), Jesus says that within a few days they will be baptized, and *"when the Spirit comes"* on them, they will receive power. So it is possible to receive a touch of the Spirit, the promise of the Spirit, without the fullness of the baptism of the Spirit. It is beautiful to have Jesus breathe on us, but don't you want the baptism?

Power to witness (Acts 1)

Here we are on the mountain, with Jesus' last words before his ascension:

⁴ On one occasion, while he was eating with them, he gave them this command: "Do not leave Jerusalem, but wait for the gift my Father promised, which you have heard me speak about. ⁵ For John baptized with water, but in a few days you will be baptized with the Holy Spirit."

⁶ Then they gathered around him and asked him, "Lord, are you at this time going to restore the kingdom to Israel?"

⁷ He said to them: "It is not for you to know the times or dates the Father has set by his own authority. ⁸ But you will receive power when the Holy Spirit comes on you; and you will be my witnesses in Jerusalem, and in all Judea and Samaria, and to the ends of the earth."

The disciples still do not have any concept of what that baptism would be like. They are still thinking about an earthly kingdom, but Jesus is talking about something out of this world, something he compares with John's baptism. It will be God's sovereign work; he says, "*You will be baptized.*" It was God's will for them, and it is his will for you as well. It is God's promise for us, and it is important to receive that power to be able to serve God.

Many still want to establish a "Christian" kingdom here on earth, and are very concerned about details of Christ's second coming, but it is best to leave those things in the Father's hands. What is important is God's power to testify about Jesus. There are two results of the baptism that Christ mentions here:

- We will receive power, to testify, preach, and do Jesus' works; God's supernatural power will flow through us.
- We will be his witnesses, preaching the good news to everyone. We should be involved not only in our local congregation, but also in extending his kingdom to the ends of the earth. That may mean going physically, praying, or supporting the mission work of the church with our finances.

What is your experience of the Spirit like?

The Bible says much more about the Spirit, but this is Jesus' teaching. Jesus asks his Father to give you the Spirit, but you can also ask him. Jesus said in Luke 11:13:

"If you then, though you are evil, know how to give good gifts to your children, how much more will your Father in heaven give the Holy Spirit to those who ask him!"

God wants to give you his Spirit! Ask him for it!

23

Will You Enter the Kingdom?

Matthew 25

When we moved to Costa Rica, I thought I had everything in order for my dog, an American Staffordshire terrier. I went to the vet and got all the required documents. However, in the San José airport, after a long day of travel, with all our luggage and the dog still in his kennel, they said he could not get in. The document lacked the seal of the authorities in New York. We started to pray, and God did a miracle: The man conferred with his superior, and they allowed him in, with the promise that the next time, I would have the required seal.

It is one thing for my dog to be denied entry. I could still get the necessary documents, or go back to the US or another country. A big pain in the neck, but I would not lose my dog. Far worse to be surprised when I come before God's throne, or see my wife, my mother, or my son there on judgment day. There are only two alternatives: enter the glory of heaven or be sent to the eternal fires of hell. I cannot go back and correct my mistakes and come back another day. It is possible to have a firm assurance that I am saved, but some passages of the Bible make me think there will be surprises. What exactly does it mean to be saved? In this book, we have studied the culture of the kingdom, but what do I have to do to enter it?

Another "Sermon on the Mount"

One day during holy week (probably Wednesday), just before his crucifixion, Jesus was in the temple with his disciples—probably the Twelve, although there could have been others. They were very impressed with the temple buildings:

Jesus left the temple and was walking away when his disciples came up to him to call his attention to its buildings. "Do you see all these things?" he asked. "Truly I tell you, not one stone here will be left on another; every one will be thrown down."

As Jesus was sitting on the Mount of Olives, the disciples came to him privately. "Tell us," they said, "when will this happen, and what will be the sign of your coming and of the end of the age?" (Matt. 24:1–3)

Aside from the Upper Room Discourse (John 14–16), this is Jesus' last recorded teaching. He finished chapter 24 with these words:

[42] "Therefore keep watch, because you do not know on what day your Lord will come. [43] But understand this: If the owner of the house had known at what time of night the thief was coming, he would have kept watch and would not have let his house be broken into. [44] So you also must be ready, because the Son of Man will come at an hour when you do not expect him.

[45] "Who then is the faithful and wise servant, whom the master has put in charge of the servants in his household to give them their food at the proper time? [46] It will be good for that servant whose master finds him doing so when he returns. [47] Truly I tell you, he will put him in charge of all his possessions. [48] But suppose that servant is wicked and says to himself, 'My master is staying away a long time,' [49] and he then begins to beat his fellow servants and to eat and drink with drunkards. [50] The master of that servant will come on a day when he does not expect him and at an hour he is not aware of. [51] He will cut him to pieces and assign him a place with the hypocrites, where there will be weeping and gnashing of teeth.

Jesus continues in chapter 25 with three scenarios to prepare us for that day and ensure that there are no surprises. When the Bible says something three times, it is important (like "Holy, holy, holy"). There is a message of eternal consequence here.

The parable of the ten virgins

¹"At that time the kingdom of heaven will be like ten virgins who took their lamps and went out to meet the bridegroom.

These are parables; they help us understand what the kingdom is like, although things do not happen exactly as described here. The Gospels are full of teaching about the kingdom. Jesus said the kingdom is within us (Lk. 17:21); it is already here on earth. The kingdom is present wherever Jesus reigns: In my life, my home, or my church. We want to extend the kingdom and its values throughout the world. We will never experience the fullness of the kingdom until Christ comes, when every knee will bow and every tongue confess that Jesus Christ is Lord. He will reign, and we will reign with him. But first, we have to make sure we are in the kingdom.

In this parable, it is obvious that Jesus is the bridegroom. We know that the church is the bride, but the bride is never mentioned. These virgins are probably bridesmaids—in this parable, Jesus needs a group to make his point, so they represent us as believers. They have gone to the wedding—an elaborate, week-long affair for the Jews—and are all waiting for the announcement of the groom's arrival. They had all expected to go in; he was not going to choose some and reject others. We all have the chance to be part of this great wedding; there is no competition between us.

They are virgins who have saved themselves for the groom. As we think about Jesus' return, we go to meet him with the expectation of entering his presence. We all have our lamps. We are pure and innocent. When Jesus walked this earth, he called prostitutes, forgave an adulteress, and received anyone who came to him, but in this parable, we are all virgins (and all women!). We leave everyone and everything else behind so we can be with Jesus.

Are you foolish or wise?

So far, everything looks great, but then Jesus says:

² Five of them were foolish and five were wise.

The Amplified Bible expands on those words: Thoughtless, silly, and careless, or far-sighted, practical, and sensible. We all like to think we are wise, but Jesus says that half of them (and of us?) are foolish. Why?

³ The foolish ones took their lamps but did not take any oil with them. ⁴ The wise ones, however, took oil in jars along with their lamps.

That is the only difference: The foolish virgins did not take extra oil with them. Their lamps already had oil, and in their experience, that would generally be enough. However, they were not thinking very well and had not planned for all the possibilities.

Maybe they ignored that gentle voice of the Spirit telling them to take extra oil. I am sure you have experienced that: You leave the house in the morning and an inner voice tells you to take an umbrella. But the sun is shining, and you are sure it is not going to rain, so you ignore the voice of the Spirit. When you leave work, it is pouring, you get soaked, and end up sick.

Or maybe a wise virgin warned a foolish one: "You need to bring extra oil," and she responds: "You always worry about everything. Just trust God," and she paid no attention.

Oil and light

Oil is a symbol of the Holy Spirit. They already had oil in their lamps, but they did not have an abundance of it. You can receive a touch of the Spirit in a worship service to fill your lamp, but when that fire goes out in the darkness that surrounds you, when the oil runs out by Tuesday, you no longer have the fullness of the Spirit. God wants to teach you to walk in the fullness of the Spirit, with your jar full, ready for any situation.

We are also the light of the world. Jesus may have purposely chosen lamps to remind us that we always need to be ready to shine his light in the darkness of this world.

The groom arrives

⁵ The bridegroom was a long time in coming, and they all became drowsy and fell asleep.

They were anxiously waiting, but the groom came late. Nobody said: "I'm tired. I'm going home to get some sleep. I'll come back in the morning." They persevered and stayed together. None of them was watching; they all fell asleep, but Jesus doesn't condemn them for sleeping. So far, everything is good.

⁶ "At midnight the cry rang out: 'Here's the bridegroom! Come out to meet him!'

Somebody was watching, because finally the excited cry ran out that he had arrived. Very late! Unexpectedly!

7 "Then all the virgins woke up and trimmed their lamps.

Everyone is awake and preparing their lamps, confident of getting into the wedding.

Just one problem

8 The foolish ones said to the wise, 'Give us some of your oil; our lamps are going out.'

It shouldn't be an issue. They are Christians; they are supposed to share. Aren't we all part of the same body, helping each other? That is usually true, but not always. There are times when we have to take care of ourselves and our relationship with Christ. Each person is responsible before Christ for their own decisions. Each one needs their own lamp; in this case, the light of your friend's or brother's lamp will not help you.

9 "'No,' they replied, 'there may not be enough for both us and you. Instead, go to those who sell oil and buy some for yourselves.'

They were not just wise to bring extra oil, but also to know that if they share it, no one will have enough. The good news is that even the foolish virgins have money, and somehow they expect to find someone selling oil at midnight. It's a hassle, but there is still hope they can make it to the wedding. After all, isn't that what Jesus is all about? Redeeming us and fixing our mistakes? They are good girls; they were not out partying or involved in any kind of "sin."

10 "But while they were on their way to buy the oil, the bridegroom arrived. The virgins who were ready went in with him to the wedding banquet. And the door was shut.

I don't know you

Just as the girls were out buying their oil, the bridegroom arrived. The ones who were ready went in with him and didn't bother to tell him that others were on the way. The door was not left open for late arrivals. It's okay for the groom to come late, but the bride and her bridesmaids need to be ready and waiting.

11 "Later the others also came. 'Lord, Lord,' they said, 'open the door for us!'

They call him "Lord" (twice!), happy that they got their oil and confident that they will finally meet the bridegroom. But the door stays securely closed—apparently, they could not open it from outside or force it open—and there is a cruel surprise:

12 "But he replied, 'Truly I tell you, I don't know you.'

How could that be? It's not fair! He doesn't know them? They had been there, waiting for hours. It was his fault that their oil ran out. And now, for one minor detail, after years of preparation, maintaining their purity, and heeding the call to the wedding banquet, he doesn't know them? There is no second chance. They could not try again the next day. The door was shut. And Jesus says:

13 "Therefore keep watch, because you do not know the day or the hour.

Are you watching? Are you ready? Do you have your oil? Have you done everything necessary to be ready when Christ comes? Don't wait until the last minute to get your life in order!

Second scene: The parable of the talents

14 "Again, it will be like a man going on a journey, who called his servants and entrusted his wealth to them.

The man would be Jesus, going away, back to the right hand of his Father in heaven. He is the wealthy master, and he has the right to entrust his wealth to his servants.

We are God's servants. He is our master. We depend on him and should always be ready to serve him.

15 To one he gave five bags of gold, to another two bags, and to another one bag, each according to his ability. Then he went on his journey.

The King James says "talents." We have traditionally thought of talents as being abilities, something we do for the Lord, but a talent was a quantity of money. For the parable, it could be money, talents, spiritual gifts, time, or any other resource that Jesus has entrusted to us. We are stewards. The Lord gives us something, not to hold onto and use as if it were ours, but to use in his service.

This is the economy of the kingdom. The American Declaration of Independence famously states that "All men are created equal." In a sense, we are, in that we are all created in God's image and should be treated as equals. But we are not all the same. God knows the ability of each person, and the reality is that some are more capable and better educated than others. He gives to us according to our ability, and he gives us some freedom as to what we do with it. He went away, leaving us to make decisions about the best way to use what he has given us.

How they managed their talents

16 The man who had received five bags of gold went at once and put his money to work and gained five bags more. 17 So also, the one with two bags of gold gained two more.

Two of them immediately went to work and doubled their gold. They took their task seriously because they loved their master and wanted to do their best for him, even though they knew none of it was theirs.

18 But the man who had received one bag went off, dug a hole in the ground and hid his master's money.

He didn't waste it or lose it. He did not rebel and take off with it, robbing his master. He was not like the prodigal son (Lk. 15:11–32), using it on wine and women. There is no evidence of what we consider sin. He just hid it; he did nothing with it.

Settling accounts

19 "After a long time the master of those servants returned and settled accounts with them.

Someday we will all have to settle accounts with God. Do you live with the understanding that God has given you what you have, and you will have to give an account of what you have done with it?

²⁰ *The man who had received five bags of gold brought the other five. 'Master,' he said, 'you entrusted me with five bags of gold. See, I have gained five more.'*

²¹ *"His master replied, 'Well done, good and faithful servant! You have been faithful with a few things; I will put you in charge of many things. Come and share your master's happiness!'*

How great to receive the Lord's praise and hear those words: "*Well done, good and faithful servant.*" He is still just a servant; he is not granted his freedom. God is going to multiply what he has, but not with houses, cars, or more money: "*I will put you in charge of many things.*" More work, more responsibility in the kingdom, in the Lord's business. The parallel passage in Luke (19:17) says: *'Because you have been trustworthy in a very small matter, take charge of ten cities.'* In addition, he can share his master's happiness. There is a special joy that comes with knowing you have faithfully served the Lord. It doesn't mean they were not happy before, but this is a deep joy, which we will experience when Christ comes and finds us fruitful and faithful, and gives us our reward.

²² *"The man with two bags of gold also came. 'Master,' he said, 'you entrusted me with two bags of gold; see, I have gained two more.'*

²³ *"His master replied, 'Well done, good and faithful servant! You have been faithful with a few things; I will put you in charge of many things. Come and share your master's happiness!'*

Whether it is five or two doesn't really matter. God is concerned about our hearts and the effort we put into serving him, not the numbers. Both servants receive the same reward.

[24] *"Then the man who had received one bag of gold came. 'Master,' he said, 'I knew that you are a hard man, harvesting where you have not sown and gathering where you have not scattered seed.* [25] *So I was afraid and went out and hid your gold in the ground. See, here is what belongs to you.'*

He may have been jealous of the ones who received more. He resented them and did not respect, honor, or fear his master. His attitude was bad. He gives back what he was given, but he had not bothered to do anything with it. He was afraid, and when you are afraid, it is hard to think or work well.

[26] *"His master replied, 'You wicked, lazy servant! So you knew that I harvest where I have not sown and gather where I have not scattered seed?* [27] *Well then, you should have put my money on deposit with the bankers, so that when I returned I would have received it back with interest.*

[28] *"'So take the bag of gold from him and give it to the one who has ten bags.* [29] *For whoever has will be given more, and they will have an abundance. Whoever does not have, even what they have will be taken from them.*

Kingdom economy

It's not socialism, where someone in authority takes from the person who has much and gives it to someone (perhaps lazy or irresponsible) who has nothing. In the kingdom, the one who has and faithfully uses it to serve the Lord receives more. It's not capitalism either, because it is not self-centered. The capitalist wants to make a lot of money and build an impressive business, mainly for his own benefit. The Lord's faithful servant is thinking about his Lord, not himself. God wants good and abundant fruit. He cuts off the unfruitful branch, while the fruitful person receives more opportunities to serve his Lord.

Jesus would have been happy with a small effort by the third servant, depositing the money in the bank—some expression of interest and desire to please his master. But he calls this servant wicked and lazy.

Again, we think of Christians as generous, sharing what we have with others. And usually that is true. But the first two servants did not offer to help their co-worker. They did not share their money so that he would have something to give the Lord and thus save his life.

Jesus did not say: "I know you had a difficult childhood. Your father was not in your life to teach you how to work. You were abused as a boy and have emotional wounds. I am going to send you to therapy and give you another chance." No! Jesus seems downright cruel!

³⁰ *And throw that worthless servant outside, into the darkness, where there will be weeping and gnashing of teeth.'*

He does not get into the kingdom. It does not matter that he was counted among the Lord's servants and was part of his "flock." Wasting or misusing what the Lord has given us results in not entering the kingdom. He could have worked for many years; that is why the Lord entrusted him with that talent. It could have been a test. Where was his heart really at? But it does not matter what happened in the past. God's judgment is not a scale: If your good deeds outweigh your evil deeds, you are fine. No, when Christ came, just like the foolish virgins, this man was lazy and irresponsible. He is worthless to Jesus and does not get into the kingdom.

It doesn't really matter how much you have right now. The Lord is watching what you do with it. Are you faithful in small things? Then the expectation, the promise, is that God will place you over much. Are you jealous of someone in the church who has received more talents? Take care of whatever God has given you. The quantity does not matter; God is watching your faithfulness, attitude, and effort.

Third scene: The judgment of the nations

[31] *"When the Son of Man comes in his glory, and all the angels with him, he will sit on his glorious throne. [32] All the nations will be gathered before him, and he will separate the people one from another as a shepherd separates the sheep from the goats. [33] He will put the sheep on his right and the goats on his left.*

Here it is obvious: It is not a bridegroom or a master, it is the Son of Man, Jesus. He has not talked much about the end, but here he clearly says what will happen:

- He will come in glory

- All the angels will come with him
- He will sit on his glorious throne as judge
- All nations will be gathered before him
- Right there, before his throne, Jesus will decide the fate of each person. There are only two options: sheep or goats.

³⁴ "Then the King will say to those on his right, 'Come, you who are blessed by my Father; take your inheritance, the kingdom prepared for you since the creation of the world.

This is your inheritance: A kingdom. God prepared it for you at the foundation of the world. They are blessed by their Father; they are the sheep. So what are the criteria used to determine whether you are a sheep or a goat?

What the righteous did

³⁵ For I was hungry and you gave me something to eat, I was thirsty and you gave me something to drink, I was a stranger and you invited me in, ³⁶ I needed clothes and you clothed me, I was sick and you looked after me, I was in prison and you came to visit me.'

They have little to do with church or religion:

- Jesus was hungry, and they gave him food
- He was thirsty, and they gave him drink
- He was a stranger and they invited him in
- He was naked (yes, that is the word in the Greek), and they gave him clothes
- He was sick and they took care of him
- Jesus was in prison! They went to visit him.

37 "Then the righteous will answer him, 'Lord, when did we see you hungry and feed you, or thirsty and give you something to drink? 38 When did we see you a stranger and invite you in, or needing clothes and clothe you? 39 When did we see you sick or in prison and go to visit you?'

They did not do those things as part of some church program, or to earn God's favor. They were totally natural, out of a heart of love, mercy, and compassion. No mention is made of preaching or healing—they just visited him. But these simple acts are what Christ expects of us.

40 "The King will reply, 'Truly I tell you, whatever you did for one of the least of these brothers and sisters of mine, you did for me.'

Jesus knows everything you do. We all know the parable of the Good Samaritan (Lk. 10:25—37). Christ made the priest and religious man the villains of the story. Jesus is not expecting us to spend a lot of money, build big buildings, or have impressive ministries. He is pleased with a glass of cold water we give to someone thirsty.

The cursed

41 "Then he will say to those on his left, 'Depart from me, you who are cursed, into the eternal fire prepared for the devil and his angels. 42 For I was hungry and you gave me nothing to eat, I was thirsty and you gave me nothing to drink, 43 I was a stranger and you did not invite me in, I needed clothes and you did not clothe me, I was sick and in prison and you did not look after me.'

What a shock to hear these words! "Get away from me! You are cursed! You will spend eternity in the fires of hell with the devil and his angels."

44 "They also will answer, 'Lord, when did we see you hungry or thirsty or a stranger or needing clothes or sick or in prison, and did not help you?'

They call him "Lord." They were fully expecting to be among the sheep. They may have been active in church. They would have rushed to get a glass of water for Jesus! They carefully avoided the worst sins, but they ignored the most important commands: Love for God and your neighbor.

45 "He will reply, 'Truly I tell you, whatever you did not do for one of the least of these, you did not do for me.'

46 "Then they will go away to eternal punishment, but the righteous to eternal life."

We need to treat everyone as though they were Christ.

Are you going to enter the kingdom?

How is your service to the most humble, unimportant people? Do you have enough oil? Are you working with the talents God has given you? These are critical things, of eternal consequence.

We know that we are saved by our faith in Jesus and what he did on the cross to forgive our sins and restore us to the Father. The first step is confessing your faith in Christ and giving him your life, but then you have to follow him and do the good works he has prepared for you. It is a process, a pilgrimage, walking by faith in Jesus. Like every race, it is less important how you start than how you finish.

In the culture of the kingdom, you:

- Live with an expectation of the King coming and establishing his kingdom. It should be a primary focus of your life. We must always be prepared.

- Work and use the resources God has given you for his glory and the growth of his kingdom.

- Take care of the neediest and the least who are around you.

24

To the Ends of the Earth

What is the next step in walking like Jesus walked? Can you sit back, rest, and just enjoy the blessings of the kingdom now? Well, we will spend an eternity enjoying those blessings. Just like God in creation, it is time to work. The seventh day, in heaven, we can rest. We saw that we are going to do the same works Jesus did. We are going to walk in this world like Jesus walked. We have power to witness. We are salt and light. God wants to raise you up as a person of influence to bring the kingdom culture to this world: "May your kingdom come." You have a part in the answer to that request.

This world needs good leaders. Whether in the family, the business world, the government, or the church, the lack of good leaders is obvious. The leader who leads like Jesus led is going to have a supernatural impact, but will also encounter strong opposition, because the culture of a godly leader is very different than that of a worldly leader.

Get the next volume in this series to learn to lead like Jesus led.